THE TALLOW CHANDLERS OF LONDON

Volume Two

THE CROWN, THE CITY AND THE CRAFTS

Plate I.
The seventeenth-
century Parlour at
Tallow Chandlers
Hall.

From a photograph
hand-coloured by
the author.

THE TALLOW CHANDLERS
OF LONDON

Volume Two
THE CROWN, THE CITY AND THE CRAFTS

by
RANDALL MONIER-WILLIAMS

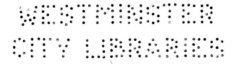
1972
KAYE & WARD LTD
IN THE CITY OF LONDON

First published by Kaye & Ward Ltd
1972

ISBN 0 7182 0900 1 / 302

All enquiries and requests relevant to
this title should be sent to the publisher,
Kaye & Ward Ltd, 194-200 Bishopsgate, London
EC2M 4PA, and not to the printer.

Printed in Great Britain by
Adlard & Son Ltd
Bartholomew Press
Dorking, Surrey

Contents

List of Plates

List of Abbreviations

Beaven	*The Aldermen of the City of London, Temp. Henry III—1908*, 2 vols (1903–13) by A. B. Beaven
Chron. Edw. I and Edw. II (*Ann. Lond.*)	*Chronicles of the reigns of Edward I and Edward II* (Vol. I *Annales Londoniensis*) ed. W. Stubbs (1882)
C.R.	*Close Rolls, Calendar of*
C.W.C.H.	*Calendar of Wills proved and enrolled in the Court of Husting, London*, ed. R. R. Sharpe, 2 Parts (1889–90)
E.M.C.R.	*Early Mayor's Court Rolls, Calendar of,* 1298–1307
Higden, *Polychron*	*Chronicles and Memorials of Great Britain and Ireland during the Middle Ages*, Polychronicon Ranulphi, Higden, Monachi Cestrensis, etc., ed. Rev. J. R. Lumby
Historical Charters	*The Historical Charters and Constitutional Documents of the City of London* by Walter de Gray Birch (1887)
L.-Bk. A, etc.	*Letter-books of the City of London, Calendar of*, ed. R. R. Sharpe
Lib. Alb.	*Munimenta Gildhallae Londoniensis, Liber Albus, etc.*, Vol. I, containing *Liber Albus* compiled in 1419 (1859), ed. H. T. Riley
Lib. Cust.	*Munimenta Gildhallae Londoniensis, op. cit.*, Vol. II, Parts I and II, containing *Liber Custumarum* with extracts from the Cottonian MS Claudius, D.II (1860), ed. H. T. Riley
O.E.D.	*Oxford English Dictionary*

P.R.	*Patent Rolls, Calendar of*
Pl. & M. Rolls	*Plea and Memoranda Rolls, Calendar of*
Riley, *Liber Albus*	*The White Book of the City of London,* compiled AD 1419 by John Carpenter, Common Clerk, Richard Whittington, Mayor. Translated from the original Latin and Anglo-Norman by H. T. Riley (1861)
Riley, *Memorials*	*Memorials of London and London Life in the XIIIth, XIVth and XVth centuries, 1276-1419,* ed. H. T. Riley (1868)
Rot. Parl.	*Rotuli Parliamentorum,* 6 Vols and Index, 1278–1508
Walsingham, *Hist. Angl.*	*Chronicles and Memorials of Great Britain and Ireland during the Middle Ages,* Chronica Monasterii S. Albani, Thomae Walsingham, quondam Monachi S. Albani, Historia Anglicana, ed. H. T. Riley

The superior numerals in the text refer to the notes in the Authorities commencing on page 118. The superior lower case letters refer to footnotes on each page.

The parishes mentioned in this and the preceding Volume are those existing in 1907 prior to the Union of Parishes Act, unless otherwise stated.

London at the turn of the thirteenth century

THE organization of our mistery with officers and ordinances, from which sprang the Livery Company of later years, can be placed, as we have seen, with reasonable accuracy in the last decade of the thirteenth century.

The nature of our men's primary occupation—that of candle-making—was such that we may have set the pace for other crafts, to whom the idea of guild-formation was still a novelty. Our raw material—the rough fat, from which tallow was made—was obtained locally from the butcher,[a] and since candles were frequently in short supply because of the scarcity of tallow, they were sold mostly in our own shops for home consumption. In our infancy the capitalist element, which in course of time was to cause the breakdown of the guild system in this country as elsewhere, was, therefore, absent. In those early days we must have been a nearly perfect model of an industrial democracy, in which every master-craftsman is ideally both manufacturer and merchant.

How to keep on good terms both with the City and the Crown was our great problem, which we shared with nearly every other mistery.

Edward I's intervention in City affairs almost from the moment when he came to the throne was profoundly disturbing to rulers and citizens alike. London merchants were largely dependent on royal patronage. The capture by Gascons and Italians of the King's favour struck a heavy blow at their means of livelihood and lowered the prestige of those merchants serving on the aldermanic

---

a   This was the usual practice. Note, however, that tallow was included with other commodities in a royal proclamation made in January 1279,[1] directing that (in aid of the repair of the walls and enclosures of the City) certain duties or 'customs' were to be payable for a period of three years by foreign merchants *bringing these commodities into the City*. The duty on tallow was 1*d*. for every wey (see page 53).

council. By the same token the admission of aliens to the freedom by the King's order thoroughly alarmed the citizens. By the custom of London only *citizens* were permitted to open shops for retail trade or to traffic with non-citizens. The encouragement of alien enterprise, although not as yet directly threatening the retail trade, appeared as a menace to this cherished monopoly.

Edward is rightly famous for his statutes, but he was much more than a legislator. He was a strong king dedicated to orderly administration and determined to rule. It did not take such a man long to discover the Londoners' shortcomings.

Fig. 1. Edward I—from a statue in the Choir of York Minster.

His reform movement under the direction of Henry le Waleys[b] must have been in full swing when, as we have seen in an earlier chapter,[c] Roger le Chaundeler and his fellow tallow-melters in Chepe were told to take 'the goods appertaining to their trade' elsewhere.

This was in the late spring of 1283.

Rokesle's Assizes—made public during that Mayor's first term of office—are known to have been revised and enlarged. Several

b   Mayor 1273-4, 1281-4 and 1298-9.
c   Vol. I, p. 51.

versions of the amended articles exist.[2] They are undated, but one detects Waleys' firm hand in their composition.[d]

They contained an order that no butcher, or wife of a butcher, should sell *tallow* or lard to a stranger for export to the parts beyond the sea 'by reason of the great dearness and scarcity that has been thereof in the City of late'.[3] This was the only regulation of direct concern to us, but the following orders, among others, were of importance to nearly everyone.

Many of the inhabitants who had gardens, particularly in the suburbs, kept pigs. Market-places and lanes must accordingly be kept clear of pigsties. Pigs must be fed in their owners' 'houses' and, if found wandering, might be captured and killed. In Rokesle's ordinance, as the observant reader will have noticed (Volume I, Appendix B), the owners had the option of feeding the animals in the open, away from the King's highway, but this involved taking them through the streets. Waleys evidently disapproved of this concession and it was withdrawn. He may have thought that there was trouble enough with the consecrated pigs of St Anthony's which, with bells round their necks, had the exceptional privilege of being permitted to roam about the City every day of the week, and once a year were allowed to enter people's houses. In 1311 it is recorded that one Roger de Winchester (or Winton), renter of the house of St Anthony in Threadneedle Street, was sworn not to lay claim to wandering pigs in the Saint's name, or to put bells on the necks of his own pigs or those of others.[4]

There were other problems requiring constant attention, with which these articles dealt.

The stream known as the Walbrook, flowing south from the marshy stretch of land beyond the walls through the centre of the City,[e] must be kept clear of filth, and the King's highway likewise. Projections from houses must be high enough to allow people on horseback to ride beneath. Rokesle's bare 9-feet clearance was

---

d   Waleys was undoubtedly responsible for the articles relating to breaches of the peace referred to later.

e   The course of the stream prior to the Great Fire of London is traced in Appendix A. The efforts to keep it clear had earlier proved to be unavailing and it had become an open sewer, which it was the duty of the owners on either side of the water-course to pave over.

wisely omitted. A later regulation required that 'pentices' should be of such a height that persons might ride 'great horses' beneath.[f]

For the convenience of neighbours, no stall must project from any house beyond 2½ feet, and it must be 'moveable and flexible'.

Bakers, butchers, brewers and taverners were all placed under strict surveillance. No baker might sell bread at his oven or in his house; he must sell it in the market. Waleys fixed the penalty for selling bread at home at 40 shillings. *No* butcher[g] might sell the skins or hides of animals in his own house or elsewhere in secret; he must carry the skins together with the flesh to the market. Brewers and taverners must sell only by stated measures sealed with the seal of the Alderman of their Ward. New penalties were imposed for breaches of this regulation.

Special attention was paid to fraudulent bakers. Any man whose bread was not up to the required standard ran the risk of being drawn on a hurdle from the Guildhall to his house through the most populous streets or, by contrast, through those streets that were 'most dirty', with the faulty loaf hanging from his neck. For a second offence he was condemned to the pillory, and for a third he must forswear the trade within the City forever.[6]

But, most important of all, Waleys' edicts contained provisions for dealing with breaches of the peace to which Rokesle's Assizes had made only a brief reference. In this he was strongly supported by the King who, on 28th November 1281, issued a writ directly entrusting to 'the Mayor and Sheriffs' the power to punish (among other offenders)[h] all misdoers walking the City by night with swords and bucklers[i] and assaulting those they met.[9] Eighteen months later, when the King was engaged in the Welsh War, Waleys was commissioned to enquire touching persons

---

f   This was in the autumn of 1297.[5]

g   Only *foreign* butchers are mentioned by Rokesle.

h   The other offenders were bakers, brewers and millers, who were said to be lax in their trades.[7] Dr A. H. Thomas observes that the document is notable not only as a commission of the peace, conferring far wider powers than those issued in the counties, but also because of this curious collocation of offenders.[8]

i   Buckler—a small round shield. In England the buckler was usually carried by a handle at the back, and used not so much for a shield as for a warder to catch the blow of an adversary, but sometimes it was larger and fastened by straps to the arm: *O.E.D.*

Fig. 2. Sword and buckler play.

guilty of homicides and felonies in the county of Surrey and in the City and suburbs of London 'and those who harbour them', and to cause their arrest.[10] In October of the same year (1283) a mandate was issued to the justices about to go on eyre[j] at the Tower 'not to molest Henry le Waleys, Mayor of London, for having during the King's absence in Wales, for the preservation of the peace and castigation of malefactors roaming about the City night and day', introduced certain *new* punishments[k] and new methods of trial and for having caused persons to be punished by imprisonment and otherwise, 'for the quiet of the City'.[11]

In May of the previous year the Mayor and Aldermen, together with Hugh Motun, the Chamberlain, had taken the significant step of directing the search of suspected persons by *trades*. Each trade was to present the names of all its members, setting out where they lived and in what Ward,[12] an order which seems to have been published not a moment too soon.

In the autumn of 1281 a great many persons had been arrested for 'divers trespasses, homicides, robberies, and assaults and for being night-walkers after curfew with swords and bucklers and for setting up games'. About seventy men in all stood their trial at this

---

j   The Court of Justices itinerant—Dr Johnson's *Dictionary*.

k   It was in 1282, according to Stow, that Waleys erected a prison for night-walkers and other suspicious persons called the Tun upon Cornhill, because it was built somewhat after the fashion of a tun (a large cask) standing on one end. Its temporary abolition, as a prison, in 1297 is referred to later (footnote *t*, p. 22).

time, the jury consisting of no less than four representatives from each of the Wards. Those found guilty of being night-walkers numbered twenty-three, including a pepperer, a barber, a tailor, a pastry-cook and five goldsmiths. Five men, including one barber, were found guilty of playing dice in taverns after curfew and three others were convicted of theft.[13] One of Waleys' edicts prohibited people from wandering about the the streets of the City after curfew rung out at Saint Martin le Grand*l* and two other churches,*m* with sword or buckler, or 'with other arm for doing mischief whereof evil suspicion might arise'. An exception was made in the case of a great lord or other substantial person of good reputation or a person of their household *going with a light to guide him*,[14] a very sensible order, seeing that no provision had yet been made for any form of street lighting.

These lists of alleged 'misdoers' are noteworthy for the number of arrested persons found not guilty and for the fact that, except (perhaps) for the thieves, every offender was released on his finding twelve 'mainpernors'*n* each of whom was willing to go bail for what was then the large sum of 100 shillings. Among the mainpernors was Matthew le Chaundeler, the central figure in Thomas' case (Volume I).

Yet another of Waleys' edicts recited that 'misdoers attached for offences, such as battery, bloodshed and other misdeeds against the peace of his lordship the King, and, upon evil suspicion taken and arrested, are often released in too light a manner, *by reason whereof others fear the less to offend*'; it was, therefore, provided that no person attached for 'a great offence' should be released without the assent of the Mayor and Aldermen,[15] a provision which was later made much more stringent.

---

l   A collegiate church of secular canons in the Ward of Aldersgate.

m   St Lawrence Jewry, on the north side of Gresham Street, south-west of Guildhall in Cheap Ward, and Barking Church, now known as All Hallows Barking, near the Tower.

n   When a man was delivered to his friends out of custody, upon their becoming bound for his appearance, such security was called 'mainprise'—taking by the hand (manucaptio)—and the sureties 'mainpernors' (manucaptores)—*Lib. Cust.*, Glossary, p. 740.

The acquittal or release on bail of so many defendants must have seemed to the King at such a time to be against the spirit of Waleys' timely ordinance. There is no reason to suppose that the Mayor was losing his nerve, but the fact remains that before very long he began to find himself in opposition to the other Aldermen, and in October 1284 he was replaced by the more sedate Rokesle.

Rokesle's third term of office lasted only eight months. There had been flagrant gaol-breaking and rioting, particularly in that area around St Paul's which was the traditional site of the Folk-moot, and the City freehold. Early in the summer following the Mayoral election the King decided to send the Treasurer, John de Kirkby, and several judges to conduct an enquiry at the Tower into the state of public order, and the Mayor, the Sheriffs, Aldermen and other City dignitaries were summoned to appear before them on 29th June 1285.[16] Rokesle disputed the right of the Commission to require their attendance except after forty days' notice. He and the other Aldermen were also indignant at the King's action in empowering the Dean and Chapter to incorporate in the Churchyard of St Paul's the historic site where breaches of the peace had so unfortunately occurred.[17] Either event may have been responsible for what followed.[o]

Rokesle delivered the Common Seal of the City to another Alderman and, according to one annalist, entered the Tower, not as Mayor, but as one of the Aldermen and 'a neighbour of the citizens' by whom he was accompanied.[19] Another annalist states that he actually resigned the Mayoralty.[20] Be that as it may, Edward retaliated at once by taking the City into his hands and appointing a Warden in the person of Sir Ralph de Sandwich, Constable of the Tower.

That autumn the great Statute of Winchester was passed. This piece of legislation makes it clear that robberies, murders, burnings and theft[21] were by no means confined to the City of London. At the same time certain statutes ordained by the King and his

---

o   It seems clear from Professor Gwyn Williams' account (derived from a document in St Paul's Cathedral Library) of what happened only nineteen days before the enquiry was due to take place that the immediate cause of the crisis was the issue of Letters Patent relating to the enclosure of the Churchyard.[18]

council were issued for the guidance of the Warden.[22] Since the
Mayor and Aldermen were apparently incapable of keeping order,
different arrangements must be made for 'the safe keeping' of the

Fig. 3. The Great Seal of Edward I.

City. It is evident that the King took this action of set purpose. His
plans must have been well laid. That he acted out of resentment or
pique, as his father had done on more than one occasion, is
unlikely. *From henceforth*, in place of the Mayor there was to be a
Warden appointed by the King, and Sheriffs and Aldermen
appointed, not by the citizens but by the Treasurer and Barons of
the Exchequer, sworn to keep watch and ward, and to maintain
the peace by night and day; and the Sheriffs, Aldermen and all the
people were to be wholly obedient to the Warden.[23]

The King's advisers thought it right to incorporate in these
statutes rules of conduct respecting the cleansing of the streets and
keeping them clear of penthouses, gutters and 'jetties of houses',
the provision of stands for carts 'shod with iron', the burning of
lime, the condition of tiles for houses, the form and manner in
which fishmongers should sell their fish, and numerous other
matters.[24] In the interests of good order the King's drastic action
in subjecting London to the direct authority of a royal officer at
least as a temporary measure had much to commend it, but it is
doubtful if this interference in the day-to-day running of the City
was either wise or necessary.

Rokesle's Assizes in the main (with Waleys' additions) were a

codification of long-established custom. The complaints about the
condition of the streets that catch the eye in the 'letter-books'
might lead one to suppose that the whole of London was in a
perpetual state of filth, but closer examination reveals that this
was not the case.[25] Undoubtedly the cleansing regulations for the
maintenance of which the Aldermen of the Wards were responsible, if judged by modern standards, left much to be desired, but
it is evident that, in the eyes of those who spent their lives there,
the machinery set up for street cleaning was satisfactory and that not
many people broke the rules. It did not seem strange to City
dwellers that a much higher standard of cleanliness should be
demanded in some parts of the City than in others. That this was
so is borne out by the penalty imposed, as we have seen, on
delinquent bakers. It is clear from that order that, while the
principal streets were kept relatively clean, others were *admittedly*
dirty. Further proof that street cleaning and the carting away
of refuse were organized is to be found in a letter from Edward III
to the Mayor of London in April 1349. There seems no doubt that
royal intervention at that time was fully justified. With the
spread of the 'great pestilence', later to be known as the Black
Death, which had reached England from Asia in August of the
previous year and the consequent depopulation that had taken
place, the City had become demoralized and cleansing activities
had deteriorated. After drawing attention to this serious state of
affairs the King ordered that London should be *cleansed of all
odours and kept clean, as it used to be in the time of preceding Mayors.*[26]

Another major cleansing problem concerned the Walbrook.
The royal officers do not appear to have thought it necessary to
deal specifically with this question. The stream was a natural
avenue for carrying away filth, if its flow could be maintained, but
it frequently became stopped up with refuse giving rise to floods.
That this danger was fully realized is plain from Rokesle's
ordinance, directing that the stream must be *freed* or, according to
Waleys, 'kept clear'.[27] Nor was there anything new in the order[28]
commanding sellers of fish and flesh not to throw dirty water onto
the pavement, but to have it carried to the Thames. There were
householders who could not resist casting refuse into the King's

B

highway, a practice which had long been frowned upon. For sanitary reasons the killing of beasts in the City created difficulties of its own but, as was the case with the general cleansing regulations, the impression that butchering offences were so common as to cause widespread inconvenience appears to have little foundation in fact.[29]

In such matters as wandering about the streets at night with evil intent and kindred offences, the King was, as we have seen, on firmer ground. Sterner measures and heavier penalties were called for.

'Forasmuch as *fools* who delight in mischief, do learn to fence with buckler', declared the new order, 'and thereby are the more encouraged to commit their follies, it is provided and enjoined that none shall hold a school for, nor shall teach the art of, fencing with buckler, within the City, by night or by day, and if any so do, he shall be imprisoned for forty days.' Waleys' edict requiring

Fig. 4. Sword dance (Royal MS. 14 E iii).

the detention of those found guilty of 'great offences' was replaced by an order that no malefactor should be released without the Award of the Warden (or Mayor) unless his trespass be *very small*, and only then if 'good and solemn mainprize' be taken. To deal with the menace of persons of ill repute, using no craft or 'merchandize', becoming innkeepers, it was provided that no man 'of foreign lands' should acquire the status of a hosteler or innkeeper until admitted to the freedom of the City 'on good testimony from the parts whence he came'.[30]

In 1289 Edward issued an order to 'the keeper and Sheriffs of London'[31] to cause renewed proclamation to be made in the City prohibiting anyone preparing himself for arms while the King was out of the realm.[p] Three years later a writ was addressed to the Warden, Ralph de Sandwich, commanding him to cause to be arrested and safeguarded in prison all misdoers and disturbers of the King's peace, homicides, robbers, incendiaries, etc. in his 'bailiwick',[32] but without any express authority either to try or to punish the offenders. This lack of punitive powers bred trouble, and when the 'statutes' were confirmed in about the year 1294 a clause was added that thenceforth no officer should be 'complained of' for inflicting punishment, unless he should have acted of open malice or for revenge.[33]

In the autumn of 1290 London had regained the right to elect its Sheriffs;[34] thereafter Edward experienced stiffening resistance from the City. His expulsion of the Jews—supported though it was by the majority of the nation—had forced him to resort to the Lombard merchants, making him more unpopular than ever with the citizens. His difficulties were rendered all the greater by war with Philip the Fair of France and trouble both with Wales and Scotland.

With the threat of invasion, special precautions became necessary for protecting the City against attack. Accordingly, in Christmas week 1294 an ordinance was made by the Warden (John le Breton),[q] Sheriffs and Aldermen for patrolling the streets by night, the first night by the Warden and Sheriffs themselves and their clerks and serjeants, with horses and arms; but this was not to relieve the Aldermen of their duty of setting the watch in

---

p   Going with horses and arms in the realm and making congregations or assemblies publicly or privately were also forbidden 'under pain of grievous forfeiture'. This was the first of a series of commissions to the counties, requiring only that *inquests* should be held and that offenders should be apprehended for trial by others.

q   John le Breton was appointed to succeed Ralph de Sandwich in 1289. The latter served again from 1289 to 1292. Breton served a second term from 1293 to 1298.

their Wards as usual.[35] We can be sure that our men were very busy at this time supplying candles for the lanterns.

On the Wednesday in Easter week 1296 Edward sent a writ of Privy Seal bidding the citizens to assist the King's son, Edward of Caernarvon, in guarding the south coast,[36] and on the following day this mandate was executed at an assembly of Aldermen and more than fifty leading citizens, among whom we find, as we should expect, the name of Matthew le Chaundeler. John le Chaundeler, who could be one of several chandlers of that name, was also there. This assembly granted for themselves 'and the whole Commonalty' that twenty horses (a number which was afterwards doubled) caparisoned with their belongings should go with Sir Edward to the sea ports, there to remain with him for four weeks, each horseman receiving 20 marks for his expenses.[37]

The King's domestic policy at this time was dictated by the need for men and money with which to prosecute the French

Fig. 5. Edward I as a warrior.

War. Money must be raised by taxing laymen and clerics alike and men must be compelled to fight abroad and to fight, if necessary, away from the King's side. London, as might be expected, supported the baronial party led by the two earls, Bohun and Bigod,[r] in their resistance to taxation without a *quid pro quo*.

Edward sailed for Flanders late in August 1297 leaving his thirteen-year-old son as Regent. In the third week of September the Warden and Aldermen were summoned to appear before the Prince Regent and his Council at the Palace of the Bishop of London, near St Paul's, when renewed instructions were given for the safe keeping of the City, including a direction that *all names of trades* should be put in writing.[38] The keeping of the gates[s] was, nevertheless, entrusted to the Wards, as it had been earlier that year,[39] and the guarding of the water of the Thames was given to those Wards nearest the river.[40]

Fig. 6. Baynard's Castle, on the river, south of Thames Street in Castle Baynard Ward.

---

r Humphrey de Bohun, Earl of Hereford, the constable, and Roger Bigod, Earl of Norfolk, the marshal.

s The principal gates were seven in number, namely, Aldgate, Aldersgate, Bishopsgate, Cripplegate, Newgate, Ludgate and the gate of London Bridge.

By October Edward had been forced to agree to the widespread demand for a 'Confirmation of the Charters', calling for an undertaking to observe the provisions of Magna Carta and for their regular publication in return for the massive financial aid which he required.[41] The collapse of the royal régime in the City was then only a matter of weeks.[42] Had it not been for the national crisis the experiment of holding the City under a Warden might have continued at least to the end of the reign. But the defensive position into which Edward had been driven on a much wider front did not permit of a hostile London.

On 30th November[43] the Warden announced to an assembly of the Aldermen, Sheriffs and six of the better and more discreet men of each Ward that he had been ordered to keep the City and all the liberties and ancient customs of the same unharmed *as of old*, and to bear himself in all things *as if he were Mayor*, although retaining the name of Warden until further orders from the King, who was staying in parts of Flanders, engaged in 'his war'.[t]

Nevertheless, it was not until the Wednesday in Easter week (1298), after the King's return, that the Mayoralty was restored,[44] and there was still a price to pay. The election of Edward's man, Waleys, as Mayor a few days later[45] appears to have been forced on the citizens,[u] and on the following Monday a writ was read to an assembly of the Aldermen 'and the people' informing them that the King had appointed John le Breton, his late Warden, and others to enquire into certain trespasses committed during his recent absence.[47] This was followed on 28th May by another writ presented this time by Waleys, as Mayor. Bakers, brewers and millers, it was said, 'frequently misconducted themselves in their trades', and evil-doers went about the City by night beating and maltreating men and committing other outrages and enormities.[v]

---

t   As part of the business of the meeting it was directed that the hurdles whereon bakers had recently been drawn through the City should be abolished, and the 'Tun' likewise, but neither order proved to be permanent.

u   The procedure was apparently without precedent, Waleys having resigned his aldermanry four years previously.[46]

v   As translated by Riley in his *Memorials*. Millers were also included in the order, the existing regulations (which required them to answer in weight for the corn sent to the mills to be ground) being repeated.

The King, wishing to apply a suitable remedy for these things and to strike the offenders and others with fear of offending, ordered the Mayor and Sheriffs to castigate such bakers, brewers and evil-doers by bodily pains *and other torments* at their discretion. These things and all others pertaining to the office of Mayor and to the preservation of the King's peace they were to cause to be observed 'inviolably'.[48]

It took nearly another year to obtain a final settlement. Not until April 1299 did the citizens obtain a confirmation of their charters,[w] for which they were compelled to pay the sum of 2,000 marks.[50] The next thing was to get rid of Waleys, in which the Aldermen were successful that autumn.[51]

Between 1298 and 1305 many cases of assault of the 'sword and buckler' type are reported in the *Early Mayor's Court Rolls*, of which the reader will find a selection in Appendix B. The election of Richer de Refham, another strong Mayor, in October 1310 was the signal for a further 'round-up' of misdoers, tres-passers and night-walkers.[52] Among numerous convictions may be mentioned the case of John le Lorymer,[x] declared to be a 'common bruiser' and committed to prison. His brother Roger, convicted of a like offence, was more fortunate. He was mainprised by William le Chaundeler, of whom more anon, and, after a short time in prison, was set free. Master Roger le Skirmisour[y] was found guilty of keeping a fencing school for divers men, and enticing thither the sons of respectable persons, so as to waste and spend the property of their fathers and mothers upon bad prac-tices. Of two brothers indicted for being 'roarers',[z] one was found to be 'a good man and true', the other was convicted.

---

w   The charter dated 17th April 1299 is still preserved at the Guildhall.[49]

x   Lorymer, lorimer or loriner—a maker of bridle bits, etc.

y   The fencer, or fencing master (Riley).

z   The terms 'roarer' and 'roaring-boy', signifying a riotous person, were still surviving in Shakespeare's day and probably even later (Riley).

It is with a sense of relief that we notice the acquittal of Robert Delle,[aa] 'chandeler', indicted in Cripplegate Ward as a bad character,[53] but truth to tell, these early chandlers (unless we are much mistaken) were among the most law-abiding of men. There were naturally a few black sheep. Witness the case of a chandler,[bb] convicted in the 'nineties of using 'opprobrious words' towards the King's serjeant, a charge which he 'straightly denied', alleging that the Aldermen who tried him were hostile.[55] In 1321, in a case in which the younger William de Manhale (Volume I) was a juror, one Hamo le Chaundeler was found guilty of being a disturber of the King's peace and an abetter of certain persons known as 'fripperers',[56] convicted of unlawfully exposing old clothes and other wares for sale by night on Cornhill.[cc] Over fifty years later—in 1375—a chandler named William Bole (of whom we shall hear more later) was charged with maliciously throwing oyster shells and other refuse on the Mayor's serjeant and committed for this and other offences to prison.[58] The most serious offence, in the eyes of the law, was in 1343, when Thomas of York, chandler, was convicted, with two other men (all three of them found to be paupers), of stealing a roll of rayed (or striped) cloth valued at 41 shillings; and the culprits, having been caught with the 'mainour'—that is to say, the stolen goods in their possession—were sentenced to death.[59] The case of Walter de Waldegrave (Volume I), in the Mayor's Court in 1305, should perhaps be mentioned because the record is sandwiched between two cases of assault. Walter, described on this occasion as a 'smeremogger' (or grease merchant), and three co-defendants had judgment given against them 'by default', but neither the charge

---

aa   Or atte Delle. He was one of those chandlers admitted to the freedom in a group in the citizen-drive of 1309 (Volume I).

bb   William le Chaundeler. Surely a different person from the 'mainpernor' of that name (supra). There was yet another William in this era, known as William 'de la Chaundelerie', in trouble with the law, but he was probably a member of the royal household and not a citizen of London.[54]

cc   In other words, holding an 'evecheping'—a practice expressly forbidden as tending to foster deceit.[57]

nor the penalty is stated.[60] It is possible that a chandler here and there may have gone unnoticed, and a few recognizable cases of dishonest trading, as distinct from acts of violence, remain to be mentioned, but even so our list of 'misdoers' is commendably short.

Fig. 7. A Frippery.

The growing power of the crafts

As we have seen, one result of Edward I's stern rule in the City was to sting the crafts into action. The Commonalty or 'Commons' of the City, sitting with the Mayor and Aldermen as an administrative assembly or 'congregatio' in the outer chamber of Guildhall, were beginning to acquire a 'juridicial personality' of their own. In Richer de Refham, they found a staunch supporter, and two years later, in the Mayoralty of his immediate successor, John de Gisors, the third, we see the *crafts* climbing onto the bandwagon.

On the Friday before the Feast of St Nicholas (6th December 1312), there came to the Guildhall the Mayor, many of the Aldermen and good men of 'the Commonalty of every mistery'[a] to treat of certain articles *for the Commonalty*, when a list of grievances was submitted and certain articles were proposed 'for the common weal'.[1]

The petition commenced with the exhortation that peace and concord should be nourished and preserved throughout the City by neighbourly unity, a sentiment which was certain to find an echo in high places, considering the parlous condition into which the Kingdom had fallen since Edward II's accession to the throne. The King had made it clear that he had little intention of carrying out the reforms embodied in the Ordinances to which he had so recently given his reluctant assent; Thomas, Earl of Lancaster and his associates had openly taken up arms, and by August civil war had seemed on the point of breaking out.

There were three grievances of immediate concern to the

---

a The word used here is 'officio' (or '*craft*', as it is generally understood) but, in this context, Dr Sharpe is undoubtedly right in rendering it as 'mistery'.

Fig. 8. Edward II—from the tomb at Gloucester.

meeting. The complaint was made that the Aldermen were not sufficiently diligent in carrying out their duties.[b] The petitioners also complained of extortion committed upon those bringing victuals to the City by Sheriffs, Clerks and Serjeants. It must have taken courage to raise these issues, but it seems that both pleas were accepted. Particular objection was taken to a merchant stranger and his servant having been admitted to the freedom by favour of 'certain great men' and contrary to the will of the good men of the trade which these two applicants followed. This problem was amicably settled by their voluntary disclaimer and surrender.

The statement of these grievances by the crafts is clear proof of their rapid advance in the matter of fifty years from comparative obscurity to organized opposition. The formulation of the following articles was of even greater significance.

It was said, by way of introduction, that owing to their youth many citizens were not sufficiently instructed in the ancient laws,

---

b   The proceedings for the election of Aldermen by Wards had been defined, and their powers confirmed, in June 1293 at a meeting presided over by the Royal Warden, at which 'the whole commonalty of the City' had been assembled. The Order, as printed in Dr Sharpe's *Calendar of Letter-books* (Book C, p. 11), is given in Appendix C.

franchises and customs of the City. To provide a remedy, two demands were made; first, that the duties of divers bailiffs (as well within the City as in the ports of the same) should be clarified; secondly, that the statutes and ordinances regulating the various trades and handicrafts should be duly enrolled, that once or twice a year they should be read in public assembly, and that copies should be delivered to such as desired them. Both these demands were accepted.

In stating their third and last requirement the petitioners observed that 'the City ought always to be governed by the aid of *men engaged in trade and handicrafts*'. They recited what was claimed to be an 'ancient custom', namely that no stranger, either native or foreign, whose position and character were unknown, should be admitted to the Freedom of the City until the merchants and craftsmen whose business he wished to enter had previously satisfied the Mayor and Aldermen as to his condition and trustworthiness. The whole Commonalty prayed that such 'observance' might be strictly kept, both as regards the wholesale trades and the handicrafts. The record does not state what view the meeting took of this demand, but from what we know from other sources it was probably accepted.

On the following day (Saturday) there was a further assembly of crafts, presided over by the Mayor, accompanied by nine Aldermen, the stated purpose of the meeting being to regulate and execute the affairs of the City,[2] but what those 'affairs' were we are not told. The narrator does not name the crafts, but tells us that at least four, and in some cases six, good men from *every craft* were present.

These two meetings on succeeding days appear to constitute the first general assembly of City crafts ever to have been officially convened, but it is unlikely that there was as yet any firm intention on the part of the misteries to depose the Wards from their traditional place in City government. Only about fifteen months earlier, while Refham was still Mayor, twelve good men from every Ward—in other words 'the whole Commonalty', as that phrase was understood—had assembled with the Mayor and Aldermen to issue a series of edicts, including a provision that every Alderman who refused to consult the men of his Ward, or omitted to carry out his duties in other respects, should be removed from his aldermanry.[3] This recognition of the duty owed by Aldermen to their electors, including, of course, many men of the crafts, must have seemed to the latter a great step forward, and there was more to come.

About three months later, that is to say on 20th November 1311 —little more than a year before the two craft-meetings—the Commons had virtually won control over the executive side of local government as well as certain branches of the City revenue. The Chamberlain, the Common (or Town) Clerk, the Wardens of London Bridge and other officers had all been elected by 'the good men of the Commonalty' with the evident intention that these elections should be annual.[4] It is true that the 'assent' of the Mayor and Aldermen was required, but to secure the right of election had constituted a major victory. Finally, in the third week in March 1312, at a *congregation* held in the presence of John de Gisors, the Mayor and a few Aldermen, the Commonalty had proposed a number of articles, including a provision that the City's seal should thenceforth remain in a chest, of which three keys should be kept by as many Aldermen and three by a like number of persons appointed by the Commonalty,[5] an article which was confirmed a few weeks later.[6]

Each one of these moves by the Commons brought the crafts a little nearer their goal. One of the articles proposed at the 'congregation' was that no stranger was to be admitted to the freedom of the City without the assent of the Commonalty.[7] In March 1313, at yet another craft-meeting, two Italians, holding charters of exemption from tax granted to them by the King, were admitted to the freedom in the presence of *good men of each mistery* only on condition that they swore to contribute to all the City's charges.[8]

It is impossible to say which of the leaders of our mistery were most involved in these proceedings. We know that we had in our ranks several Ward representatives, or 'Commoners'—as they were beginning to be called—from the time when records first become available, and we may well believe that there were others.

The earliest surviving list of Commoners is thought to belong to the year 1285 and to have been furnished for the use of the Royal Warden.[9] The number of representatives varies from one to three. Candlewick had two, the first name being that of Matthew le Chandler. Six years later we see him again in that position as one of the reputable men elected by 'common assent and consent' of the whole Commonalty for the City's account,[10] and this time we find also the name of Michael the Oynter (Volume I) representing Aldgate.[11] Matthew appears once more, in 1297, as the senior representative of his Ward when a tax was imposed on the citizens and other persons residing in London to discharge the debts of the City.[12] Had he lived[c] he is certain to have represented our mistery at the three craft-meetings. We do not hear of Michael the Oynter after 1291. We know something of his private life from two entries in the Letter-book[14] (see Appendix D) from

Fig. 9. Female dress, time of Edward II (Sloane MS. 346).

one of which we learn that he was separated from his wife, Gonilda, but we do not know when he died.

Walter le Chandler, who represented, with three other Commoners, the Ward of Ludgate Within and Without in 1297

---

c   His will was enrolled in 1306–7.[13]

(Volume I), may well have been included in our team, and another likely member was William le Chandler, to whom the reader was introduced in the last chapter. He was the senior representative of the Ward of Ludgate Within when Matthew was, for the third time, leader for Candlewick.[15] We hear of him first in 1288 as a witness to a deed in company with the Royal Warden, the Sheriffs, Henry le Waleys (Alderman) and Hugh Motum,[16] the Chamberlain. He appears next in the Corporation records as doing business in the City.[17] Then in 1299 he is mentioned more than once, with several other chandlers, among the many London creditors of Gascons, for whose debts the King had perforce agreed to be responsible.[18] We meet him later taking apprentices, and sponsoring others for admission to the freedom by servitude during the citizen-drive (Volume I). He resided 'without' Aldersgate[19] and as late as 1325 is seen holding the important office of Warden of the Gate, while a colleague, Hugh le Chaundeler, occupied an equivalent position at Bishopsgate.[20]

Other promising candidates were John de Chelse, John de Lyndesey, William de Manhale (the younger) and Henry le Chaundeler. The first three have already received recognition as prominent citizens (Volume I), and both Johns were among those who, in 1320, voluntarily surrendered one-half of each contributor's claim to be repaid money advanced to Edward II (so we are reminded) in the tenth year of his reign.[21] In 1318 we see the second John's name among those citizens 'of the more powerful and better class', each of whom found an armed foot-soldier to assist the King in the Scottish War.[22] Three years later when, at the King's command, a scheme was drawn up for the City's defence against the 'Contrariants',[23] and the keys of the several gates were put in commission, those of Newgate, in Farringdon Ward, were entrusted to the second John and another member of the same Ward.[d] Henry le Chaundeler was another of those lucky creditors of Gascons whose claims were settled by Edward I. In 1310 his

---

d   John de Lyndeseye and Roger Hoseboude (the other member mentioned here) represented (with others) the Ward of Farringdon in 1317[24] and both are named as witnesses with Nicholas de Farendone 'Mayor and Alderman of the Ward' to a lease of property in the Ward.[25]

name appears as one of five Commoners who, with the rest of the 'good men of the Ward of Vintry', presented John de Gisors (later to become Mayor) as their Alderman[26] for admission to the aldermanic council, or 'Court of Aldermen' as it was beginning to be known.[e] Judging from his will he appears to have been a man of means.[f] For good measure we may note that, among his lesser gifts, he gave his stepson the choice of 100 shillings' worth of morters[g] or candles.

The reform movement seems to have been at its peak in the spring of 1313 and thereafter to have gone into a temporary decline. For six years little is heard of the crafts. The reaction of the aldermanic council to what must have seemed the excessive ambition of the misteries can be seen in the resolution of 28th September 1313 passed at a meeting of the Mayor, Aldermen and Commonalty for the declared purpose of avoiding 'certain perils' which might arise at the election of Sheriffs. The order that 'in future' there should be summoned to the election every year *the better men of each Ward*[30] was no more than a statement of established practice, for these elections had always been 'managed'. The same can be said of the royal writ published by the Council in July 1315 directing that mayoral as well as shrieval elections should be conducted 'in the accustomed manner', that is to say *by the Aldermen* and others of the more discreet and powerful citizens.[31] (See Appendix E.) The resolution of 1313 is seen from the record[32] to have been strictly enforced at the election of the following year. For the mayoral election in 1315 the Aldermen issued a proclamation that no one should be 'so daring nor so hardy' as to appear, unless he be Mayor, Sheriff or Alderman, or belonged to 'the better sort' of the City, who by the officers of the said City had been *specially summoned* to come there, or who had business to be there, on pain of imprisonment of his body.[33]

---

e   Administrative business was conducted by the Court in the 'Inner Chamber'. Judicial business was conducted in the 'Mayor's Court'.

f   He is described in his testament as Henry le Chaundeler de Garlekhuth, or Garlickhithe (in Vintry Ward).[27] He could be the same person as Henry le Chaundeler, beadle of John Wade (Volume I), who appears at a later date (1307) to have been one of the latter's executors.[28] Wade was a wealthy Alderman in the grain trade.

g   Probably thick candles, used especially as night-lights (Volume I, p. 21).[29]

Plate II. 1. A Baker at the Oven, temp. Edward I 2. A Baker drawn on the Hurdle with the faulty loaf attached to his neck temp. Edward I 3. The Pillory, 1 Edward III 4. The Pillory 6 Richard II.
From the Assisa Panis, 21 Edw. I–16 Henr. VI, preserved at Guildhall. By the courtesy of the Guildhall Library, London.

In their struggle for power the misteries had gone too far but, in the summer of 1319, the craft movement undoubtedly recovered some of the lost ground. With the rise to power of Alderman Hamo de Chigwell—a wealthy fishmonger, soon to become Mayor—the Commons, with the crafts in the van, returned to attack. His immediate predecessor, John de Wengrave, a professional administrator, first elected Mayor in 1316 while still holding the newly created office of Recorder, had become increasingly unpopular. He had been re-elected for the second time in October 1318 only by procuring letters from the King (so it was said) and by consent of 'certain persons of influence, against the will of the Commons'.[34]

After the loss of Berwick in April 1318, the King had been compelled to prosecute the Scottish War with greater vigour, and with this object in view the Court had moved in October to York, the second largest city in the Kingdom. From York Edward issued

Fig. 10. Attack with battering rams on the walls of a besieged town.

Letters Patent dated 8th (or 18th) June 1319 sanctioning new articles submitted by the Mayor, Aldermen and the Citizens of London,[35] as well as an Inspeximus Charter[h] of even date[i] confirming the City's liberties.[36] Among the twenty articles was an ordinance which was very soon to become an essential part of the City's constitution, although not all the others proved to be permanent. No alien was to be admitted to the freedom except in the Husting[j] and with the assent of the Commonalty, unless he belonged to some mistery or trade, and no man of English birth and particularly no English merchant who followed a mistery or trade was to be admitted except on the security of six honest and sufficient men of that mistery, a rule which applied also to aliens.[37]

There were two other provisions of which the reader is invited to take note.

The first[k] was a restatement of an established practice. Everyone living in the City and wishing to enjoy its liberties and customs must be in 'lot and scot' and partake of all burdens for maintaining the state of the City and the freedom thereof, and all persons being of the freedom of the City and living outside the City, and either by themselves or their servants 'exercising their merchandise' within the City, must be in lot and scot with the Commoners of the City 'for their merchandises', or else be removed from their freedom.[l] In 1354 enquiries were made of the Mayor and Chamberlain as to whether Robert de Manhale and William de St Albans, both chandlers whom we shall meet later, were in scot and *geld*.[m] On searching the Rolls and Memoranda in the Chamber of the Guildhall it was found that Robert had been

---

h   A charter in which the grantor testifies that he has inspected an earlier charter, which he recites and confirms.

i   Said to have cost the City the sum of £1,000.

j   '*Nisi in Hustengo*'. At this date the 'Husting' was still the supreme court of the City.

k   Articles 9 and 10.

l   The precise meaning of the phrase 'lot and scot' is not known. According to Riley by 'scot' was meant the payment of contributions and taxes, 'lot' being the assessment thereof in due proportions.[38] The question of what was meant by 'paying scot' was debated before the Court of Aldermen in 1719, when the Court came to the conclusion that the term meant a general contribution to *all* public taxes.[39] The addition of 'geld', or the substitution of that word for 'lot' (as in the next example in the text), creates a further complication.

m   Lat. 'geldum' or 'gelda', Anglo-Saxon 'gild' = tax, impost. Hence 'guild', a fraternity whose members contributed to a common fund.[40]

admitted to the freedom in 1325 and William in 1338, and that both were in scot and geld.[41]

The second provision[n] has a special interest for our Company, as we shall see later. The Keeping of London Bridge, and the profits belonging to the bridge, were to be committed to two honest and sufficient men of the City other than the Aldermen, and these men were to be chosen by the Commonalty.

As if to advertise their newly acquired importance, the misteries now began to array themselves in liveries. In the words of the chronicler, 'a good time was about to begin',[42] but events were to prove him over-optimistic. Hamo de Chigwell was elected Mayor in October 1319[43] in the midst of the bitter national conflict which was to result in the deposition and murder of a king whom none could trust. He was followed next year by Nicholas Farndone, 'all the Commoners sitting in Guildhall, and silence being demanded for the election'.[44] Early in 1321 the memorable 'Iter'[o] instituted by Edward commenced at the Tower and no sooner was it under way than Farndone was deprived of his office and a Royal Warden appointed in his place.[46] In May the citizens were again permitted to elect a Mayor and Chigwell was chosen for a second time,[47] but their liberties do not seem to have been fully restored until after the King had fled to Wales, when on 6th November 1326 a writ was received from 'Edward, the king's first born son, guardian of the realm',[48] announcing the restoration of the Mayoralty.[p]

That same month saw the crafts again meeting as a body in Guildhall, assuming that the order directing them to assemble was duly carried out, in which case it seems to have been an early experiment in electing men of the misteries as Commoners.

The way in which the entry in the corporation records is introduced to us is a sign of the times. 'The First Proclamation after the

---

n   Article 17.

o   The Iter lasted for over twenty-four weeks, its professed object being to examine into unlawful 'colligations, confederations, and conventions by oaths' said to have been formed in the City.[45]

p   The intervening events are shortly related in a footnote on p. 214 of Dr Sharpe's Calendar of Letter-book E.

beheading of the Bishop of Exeter' it reads.[49] Walter Stapleton
was one of the favourites of Edward II and shared their unpopu-
larity. After the landing of Queen Isabella with Roger Mortimer
and young Edward at Harwich in September (1326) Stapleton
was responsible for publishing bulls of excommunication against
the King's enemies. When the City rose on 15th October he was
caught making his way to St Paul's Church, where he was met by
a crowd, dragged from his horse and beheaded in Chepe.[50]

The main object of the proclamation was the maintenance of
the King's peace. In order to avert perils and slanders from so good
a city, which was 'a mirror to all England', no man of whatsoever
condition was to be so bold as to rob or 'riffle' or take goods
against the will of the owner, in the City and outside, under
penalty of life and limb. Each Alderman was to keep watches in his
Ward as usual and no man was to go armed by night or day save
officers and other good men assigned to keep watch; no man was

Fig. 11. Watchmen (early seventeenth century) according to Decker.

to seek vengeance by reason of any past quarrel, but those who felt
themselves aggrieved were to sue by way of law. Then came the
two articles which particularly concerned the crafts. First, *certain
men of each mistery* were to be chosen by the assent of the same
misteries to come to Guildhall, where the Mayor and Aldermen,
together with these chosen representatives, were to treat and
ordain on the needs of the City, 'in salvation of all men, denizens

and strangers, dwelling or repairing thither.'q Secondly, the good men of the City who had their apprentices, hired men or servants working with their hands or trading, were to cause them to work or trade *as they were wont to do*, and to inform the Mayor, officers and other good men of the City of any that were rebellious, and such men were to be duly punished as a warning to others.

Chigwell was in his third term as Mayor at this time, but Mortimer did not trust him. On 15th November he was removed from office and Richard de Betoyne (or Bethune) was elected in his place.[51] The Londoners had by now decided that Edward II must go and on 12th January 1327 letters were sent by the Mayor, the Aldermen and Commonalty of London to the Archbishops, Bishops, Earls, Barons and other great men asking whether they were willing to be 'in accord with the City' and to swear to maintain the cause of Queen Isabella and Edward her son, to crown the latter and to depose his father for his frequent offences against his oath and his Crown.[52] On the following day the magnates came to Guildhall and took an oath to the new King.[53] It seems certain that many men of the crafts were deeply involved in this dramatic and unprecedented move.r

The Londoners were well rewarded for the part they had played in putting Edward III on the throne. On 6th March 1327, less than six weeks after his accession, the young King granted his first charter 'for the bettering of our City, and for the good and laudable services often done to us and our progenitors by our beloved mayor, aldermen and commonalty'. The liberties granted by former charters, particularly Magna Carta ('the great charter of the liberties of England'), were confirmed; the ancient privilege of not being compelled to plead (or to be impleaded) outside the City walls, on which the citizens set great store, was endorsed; and never again was the City to be taken into the King's hands.[55]

---

q   The remaining words requiring that 'the matters thus *ordained* by them' were to be shown to the Commonalty 'before they be completed' can be explained only if the assembly is regarded as no more than an *ad hoc* meeting of the misteries in committee.

r   Dr A. H. Thomas goes so far as to say that the craftsmen were actually responsible for calling the meeting.[54]

In the same month the Tailors (or Tailors and Linen Armourers[s] as their guild was known at that time) received a so-called 'Charter of Liberties', and royal charters were granted to the Girdlers, Goldsmiths and Skinners giving them rights of search throughout the Kingdom.[56]

Fig. 12. The Crest of the Worshipful Company of Girdlers.

In October (1327) we are reminded of the prominent position in the City now held by the misteries as a whole. In a proclamation forbidding night-walking after curfew and the carrying of arms the following passages occur: 'aggrieved persons must not form covins,[t] but complain to *the Wardens of their misteries*, or sue at law' and '*The Wardens of the misteries* must keep their men at work and report any rebellious behaviour to the Mayor and good men of the City'.[57]

Next year the representatives of twenty-five misteries are listed as having been chosen for 'the government and instruction of the same.'[58] There are a number of notable absentees from the table, including the Armourers, Bakers, Curriers, Dyers, Fullers, Horners, Loriners, Wax chandlers and ourselves.[u] The omission

---

s   Linen armoury—the occupation of lining and quilting armour.

t   Covin—a deceitful agreement between two or more, to the hurt of another (Dr Johnson's *Dictionary*).

u   The Loriners' ordinances, as we have seen (Volume I), were very ancient. The Horners' statutes dated from 1284[59] and the Fullers' ordinances from 1298.[60] The Dyers, jointly with the Fullers, had appointed overseers of the craft in 1314[61] to replace others of earlier date. The Armourers had had their regulations recorded at the Husting in 1322.[62]

of such names as these, coupled with the fact that the folio in the Letter-book immediately following the folios on which the lists occur is seen to be blank, would alone suggest that the table is incomplete.[63]

The City took a leading part in the early opposition which gathered round Henry, Earl of Lancaster, against Mortimer's arbitrary rule, but we are not told what part the crafts played in this manoeuvre, which ended with Mortimer's arrest and execution.

When Parliament met early in March 1337 the City, with an eye to the main chance, took the significant course of making presents to the King and Queen and other magnates,[64] which were used to aid in the coming struggle with France. Later that month London was freed for a time from the provisions of a statute passed at York in 1335 permitting merchant-strangers to trade freely throughout England.[v] The gift of money doubtless helped in restoring the citizens' trade monopoly, but that was not the end of the matter. A further large sum had to be raised for this and other purposes by assessment in the Wards.[66]

In April 1338, with the outbreak of the Hundred Years War, the Mayor and Aldermen were called before the King and his Council at Westminster, and on being asked whether they would safeguard the City on behalf of the King, who was about to cross the sea, they agreed to do so. Thereupon they were commanded to submit their plans in writing within a week.[67] The scheme which met with approval provided, among other things, that men from the Wards should patrol the City day and night, that any person making cry or noise near the windows or doors of houses and shops, so as to create a riot in the City, should have forthwith 'judgment of life and limb', and that none should go armed in the City save the King's servants and those assisting them.[68]

In the autumn, to help in putting the City into 'a posture of defence', two or more men from each Ward were appointed to act as collectors of money from various religious houses and

---

v   By Charter dated 26th March 1337.[65]

others holding property in the City, but not bearing lot or paying scot.[69] In the following March arrangements were made to keep guard over the Thames by night for fear of foreign invasion, and four Aldermen were assigned to watch each night 'with good men of their Wards'.[70]

The money for the presents was borrowed from a great number of citizens, among whom were John de Westwyk 'chaundeler', Roger Chaundeler (or le Chaundeler), Robert de Manhale, Henry atte Rothe or Roche (see Appendix L, note a) and Johanna, wife of William de St Alban.[w] Among those chosen for patrol work were John de Enfeld, as a representative of the Ward of Chepe, and Arnald (or Arnold) le Chaundeler for the Ward of Bridge, and the same two men were appointed in their Wards as collectors. The names of those appointed to guard the Thames are not recorded.

The mention of John de Enfeld and William de St Alban(s) calls to mind our oynter colony in West Chepe. John atte Holme(s) de Enfeld, to give him his full name (see Appendix L, note a), was an apprentice of Matthew de Fulham, the third occupant of Roger de St Albans' eight shops in 'Oynters' Row', one of which was inherited by John from Matthew. John held this shop until 1323 when he sold it to William Danyel, alias William de St Albans, the purchaser of the other seven shops. Johanna, named above as one of the City's creditors, had recently acquired an interest in all the eight shops under her husband's will. (See sections H and J of the Guide in Volume I.) In 1337 John joined with a number of other persons living near the Great Conduit in Chepe in complaining that the Commonalty were deprived of the water owing to its being so much used by brewers, who carried it away in vessels called 'tynes'. Whereupon judgment was given to the effect that the Wardens of the Conduit were to seize such tynes and retain them 'for the benefit of the Conduit'.[72] Eight years later an ordinance was made imposing severe penalties on brewers and others using the water.[73] (Appendix F.)

---

w   Not to be confused with the William de St Albans mentioned on page 34. Johanna was in fact a widow in March 1337, her husband's will having already been enrolled.[71]

Fig. 13. The Conduit shown here is that known as 'The Standard', near the entrance to Honey Lane, north out of West Chepe. (See the western section of Leake's map—Volume I, endpaper.)

Johanna provides us with what appears to be our only link with William de Hatfeld (or Hathfeld), the seventh occupant of Roger de St Albans' shops (section K of the Guide) and his wife Emma. In 1347 William purchased from Johanna a tenement in 'Bordhawelane'[74] which he left by his will, enrolled in 1369, to Emma.[75] This lady carried on the trade of a tallow chandler, and it so happens that we have a complete inventory of her goods delivered to one Matthew Langrich, fishmonger, and Margaret (his wife), who was the Hatfelds' daughter, including candles, tallow, grease, oil, cotton, and salt.[76] (See Appendix G.) Margaret was a minor whom Matthew had married without the permission of the Court, incurring a fine of 60 shillings for so doing.[77]

John de Westwyk, Robert de Manhale and Henry atte Rothe[x]

---

[x]   Henry is described in a purchase deed of shops in Ironmonger Lane (see note 79(c), page 125) as an ointer (unctuarius), an even later use of that word than was mentioned in the case of John de Chelse (Volume I). At other times he is referred to as a chandler or chaundeler.[78]

were all property owners.[79] John was among a number of overseers appointed in 1345 to see that the watercourse of the Walbrook
was not impeded.[80] We shall be meeting Robert and Henry
again very soon, and Roger Chaundeler also, but not Arnald le
Chaundeler, of whom very little is known.[y]

We are reminded by an entry in the *Plea and Memoranda Rolls*
at this time that the manufacture and sale of tallow candles did not
represent our men's sole occupation. We have seen in Volume I
how closely candle-making was allied to the making of sauces,
and we may note from the following examples how the descrip-
tions 'chandler' and 'sauser' were sometimes used interchangeably.

In July 1298 John le 'Caundeler' (or Chaundeler), called 'le
Faukes de Reda',[z] acknowledged a small debt[84] to one Roger de
Sandwych.[aa] A few years later John de Red, '*Sauser*', and another
man of a different trade, acknowledged a debt of 10 marks,[85] for
which they entered into a recognizance. In February 1300 John le
Sauser, '*Caundeler*' and four others acknowledged a debt of
60 shillings 'current money', payable to the Abbot of Waltham,[86]
and in June of that year John 'le Caundeler' (referred to later in the
same entry as 'John, the Chandler') with one William de Chertesey,
'Caundeler', acknowledged a debt of the same amount to the
Warden of the Hospital of St Mary de Annesty (Ansty, Co.
Herts).[87] In February 1311 Reginald le Chaundeler, '*sauser*',[bb] and
three others acknowledged a debt of nearly £30 to one William
de Bidix.[89]

The historic record to which we are introduced on 26th
November 1339 runs thus:[90]

---

y   His assessment in the Lay-subsidy list of 1332 was a low one[81] and, apart from the
      references in the text, our knowledge of him seems to be limited to an entry in the
      Close Rolls recording that prior to 1337 he had been entrusted by one Robert de
      Stanes with certain charters and muniments.[82]

z   Perhaps the same man as John Fauk de Red who, in 1276, in association with
      Reginald le Chaundeler (Volume I) and others, acknowledged a debt of 20 marks for
      barley.[83]

aa   Roger is stated to be the son of '*Hugh the King's Sauser (salsarius)*'. The origin of the
      debt is not known.

bb   Not to be confused with Reginald le Chaundeler residing in the parish of St Michael
      le Quern (Volume I) who died in 1296.[88]

'The following chandlers were sworn to oversee their trade and to prevent bad liquor being put into mustard, sauces and saxifrage;*cc* for the West [of the Walbrook] John le Chaundeler of St Lawrence Lane, John de Totenham, John de Saunford, Walter Cady,*dd* [and] William de Douuegate; for the East, Roger de Clovyll, Henry de Stystede, Robert le Chaundeler of Candelwykstrate, and John le Chaundeler of Grasscherche (Gracechurch Street).'

Four years later the same men were again sworn, except for John de Saunford, who had died, his place being taken by Hugh de Chandeler of Eldefisshstret (Old Fish Street).[92]

Of these chandlers John de Totenham was probably the best known, although Roger de Clovyll (or Cloville) was also a man of means.[93] At the time of John's death in 1349 he held property in what is now called Maiden Lane and elsewhere.[94] He was one of those chosen in November 1339 to assess the men of their Wards and to levy money for presents as in 1337 'with special consideration for the poor';[95] when next March the King asked for further money by way of loan he was one of the contributors;[96] he was assessed again as a matter of course in 1346[97] when Edward was conducting his victorious campaign, made famous by the battle of Crécy and the capture of Calais.

In the 1339 levy we find, along with the name of John de Totenham, that of Robert de Manhale and, in the levies of 1340 and 1346, the names of Robert de Manhale, Roger Chaundeler and Henry atte Rothe, all contributors, as we have seen, in 1337; from which we may conclude that these four men were the leaders of our mistery at this period. We should be tempted to add a fifth in the person of John de Westwyk, who evidently died a rich man, but for the absence of his name from the Lay-subsidy list of 1332 and from the last three levies.

---

cc   Dr Thomas's note is as follows: '*non ponant falsum Licorem in senapio nec in aliis sausibus sive saxifragiis.* The root of the white meadow-saxifrage was used in the Middle Ages as a condiment, and was supposed to possess medicinal properties.'

dd   The name Walter Cady is an interlineation, indicating, perhaps, that Walter was a substitute either then, or later, for one of the other overseers.[91]

Fig. 14. The Battle of Crécy.

The name of Robert de Manhale occurs again in 1356 among the 'wealthier and wise Commoners of the City' when it was agreed to make an assessment in the Wards for the repair of two vessels in aid of the war.[98] He is called Robert de Clare[ee] in the will of John de Oxon, Rector of St Peter upon Cornhill, from whom he received a gift of land in that parish,[99] and in the will of John de Enfeld, of which he was an Executor.[100] We know he was an Executor of the will of William de Manhale the younger (Volume I),[101] who could have been his father or to whom he may have been apprenticed, it being quite common for an apprentice to take his master's name. The will itself does not appear to have survived. His own will, providing for his wife, two sons and three daughters, was enrolled in March 1360.[102]

Little else is known for certain of Roger Chaundeler, but he is probably the same person as Roger de Mymmes, chaundeler, whose will was enrolled in March 1348.[103] Roger appointed as one of his Executors his kinsman John le Chandeler in Juwerielane. If by Jewry Lane is meant St Lawrence Lane in the Jewry, as seems

---

ee   Suggesting that he came from Clare in Suffolk.

fairly certain, it is likely that both men belonged to one of the oynter colonies in the parish of St Mary Colechurch, and that Roger was a descendant of Warin de Mimmes (Volume I). From his association with the lane (if proved) it also appears that this John was the 'John le Chaundeler of St Lawrence Lane' named first in the record of searchers for the West of the Walbrook.

Henry atte Rothe was one of those men chosen in January 1348 to look into the question of putting down nuisances arising from the sale of 'small victuals and other merchandise' in the highways of Chepe, Cornhill and elsewhere.[104] By this date these thoroughfares were probably losing their earlier daily-market character and each market was becoming increasingly an emporium. Accompanying Henry atte Rothe in his investigations was William de St Alban(s) (the second), chandler, a Warden (Keeper or Master) of the Conduit in Chepe.[105] From the Wardens' account given in the Letter-book in 1350[106] he had evidently held this position for some time,[ff] apart from which we know very little about him, except that he was assessed in 1332 as a resident of the Ward of Chepe for only a modest sum[107] and that he later appears to have changed his Ward.[gg]

Fig. 15. Head-dresses, early fourteenth century (Royal MS. 14 E iii).

---

ff   Details of the expenditure for the period under review, as printed in Riley's *Memorials* with the editor's notes, will be found in Appendix H. The account ends with a plea by the Wardens for some reward for their trouble during the time that they were 'Masters'.

gg   He was summoned in July 1340 to a coroner's jury as a resident of the Ward of Cripplegate Without.[108]

When next we hear of the searches for sauces they are being conducted by the mistery of Vintners. On 7th November 1375 twelve of their men were sworn for the scrutiny of wines *and vinegar* in taverns and cellars, and to pour out in the streets whatever they found corrupt and unhealthy. The same persons were sworn to do likewise with the sauces (salisamentum) of the *chandlers*. The City boundary line between east and west is still the Walbrook, the searchers being divided into two equal parties.[109] In an entry less than a fortnight later we read that these searches were the subject of 'an ancient ordinance', which included a direction that no new wine should be placed in cellars where old wine was left and that no unsound wine, vinegar *or other sauces in chandlers' shops* should be offered for sale.[110] We learn then of one of the comparatively rare trading offences committed by chandlers. William Bole, of whom the reader has already heard, was found guilty of an unspecified breach of the regulations for which he incurred a penalty of 2 shillings. He made matters worse by resisting a distress upon his goods; and then occurred the incident of the oyster shells (page 24) with more to follow, for when the scrutineers wished to enter his house to exercise their office, he drew his knife against the serjeant and called him a 'babelbera' (gossip) and other opprobrious names.

Another search by Vintners alone for wines, vinegar and sauces took place in November 1376[111] and three years later yet another is recorded by Vintners and 'other good men', whose calling is not specified. The party on this second occasion were sworn to make a scrutiny of wine, vinegar, aysel (a type of vinegar) and *other* sauces in the cellars and shops of chaundelers *and others* and to dispose of those that were unsound in the usual manner.[112]

We shall hear before the close of the century of tallow chandlers joining in searches with Vintners and later with Salters. We return now to the 'forties.

In July 1343 we come to an entry which affords a rare instance of chandlers and wax-chandlers engaging in business together, business which, regrettably, was not, on this occasion, in the public interest, consisting as it did of mixing *fat* with the wax in wax candles and torches.[113] To remedy this evil four men, described as 'chandlers and **wax candle** makers [cirgiarii]', were sworn to 'make a scrutiny'. One of them, William atte Noke (see Appendix L, note *a*), can be identified as a 'cirger' (or wax-chandler);[114] another, Roger de Wodhull (or Wodhulle), as a chandler.[115] The identities of the other two have not been established.

In the following December we get the earliest recorded case of trade deception by tallow chandlers on their own, Bole's case coming, as we have seen, a great deal later. Over three hundred and fifty pounds of candles of false weight were found in the possession of three women and one man,[hh] resulting in the offenders being brought before the Mayor and Aldermen for trial.[117] Their treatment was surprisingly lenient, the candles 'by favour of the Mayor' being restored to the owners on the understanding that any false candles found with them in future would be confiscated. The next recorded breach of City fair-trading regulations in which one of our men was involved concerns the purchase of a cargo of *salt*, a commodity which some chandlers—competing at times with the salters—are known to have bought for resale, as well as for sauce-making. In 1354 Thomas de Mordon, chandler, was found guilty of forestalling the market. It appears that he made his purchase before market hours (the ship then being moored to the quay), paying one penny a bushel more for the salt than the current price and, thus, having cornered the whole available supply, was able to charge what he liked.[118] Another somewhat similar case in which a chandler dealing in salt was involved occurred sixteen years later. Two years after Thomas's offence— and perhaps as a result of it—an ordinance had been passed forbidding any merchant to purchase corn, malt or salt coming to the City by water in ships or boats to the 'havens' of Billingsgate

---

hh   The three ladies were all named Alice. Alice la Strengere (a stringer = a roper or corder) and Alice, late wife of Robert le Chaundeler, whose son Ralph was the fourth offender, appear to have been carrying on business together. The third Alice—married to Robert le Noreys, 'chaundeler'—seems (as does Ralph) to have been trading alone. In 1327 the Mayor and Aldermen had examined 'Ralph's body and stature' and certified that, as his father's son and heir, he was of full age and capable of disposing of rents and tenements.[116]

or Queenhithe before the merchandise had remained at the havens for three days next after its arrival, 'so that the good folk and Commonalty of the City might be able to supply their hostels and houses.'[119] On 5th December 1370 John de Sevenoke, chandler, was attached to answer the Sheriffs that, notwithstanding the ordinance, he had bought twenty-four quarters of large salt at Queenhithe for resale, which had arrived only the previous day. He admitted the offence and judgment was given that the salt be forfeited to the use of the Sheriffs.[120]

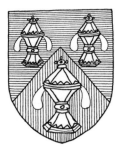

Fig. 16. The Shield of the Worshipful Company of Salters.

Plate III. The Tower in the fifteenth century.

The dawn of a new era

DURING the 'forties the Commons of the City were rapidly coming into their own, and in the first week of Lent 1347 we witness the formation of what is thought to have been the first Common Council,[1] consisting (as it does today) of Commoners in company with the Mayor and Aldermen. At a congregation of the Mayor, Aldermen and 'an immense Commonalty' the names were announced of over 130 persons chosen in their respective Wards *to come to Guildhall when warned* 'on matters affecting the City'.[a] A majority of the Wards provided six representatives. This was so in the case of Cornhill and Coleman Street, in both of which Wards the list of names is headed by a chandler, our friend Robert de Manhale for Cornhill and John de Hatfeld for Coleman Street.[3] This John, as we shall see, was one of our most prominent members.

The year 1351 saw the beginning of a novel and, as it proved, an unsuccessful experiment. In November of that year a bill was sent to thirteen of the leading misteries calling upon them to assemble their men, with instructions to cause an election to be made 'by common assent' of four good men of each *mistery*, being 'the wisest and most able to treat with the Mayor, Aldermen and Sheriffs of certain important business touching the state of the City'. The order was not carried out very strictly, the Grocers, Mercers and Fishmongers each submitting the names of six men, and the Ironmongers—one of the newer mercantile crafts—only two. The Grocers and Vintners each included an Alderman, whose

---

a   The list as printed by Riley in his *Memorials* at pages liii–lv is headed '*The First Common Council elected in the City of London*'. This assumption has been criticized on the ground that the supposed antiquity of the name rests mainly on a misinterpretation of the phrase *per commune consilium*, meaning 'by the common counsel' (of the citizens).[2]

name was accordingly struck out! The list, as entered in the Letter-
book, is introduced to us as follows:

> 'Names of those elected from the aforesaid misteries to
> attend at the Guildhall on business touching the City when
> summoned on behalf of the Mayor, Sheriffs, and Aldermen.'[4]

Notwithstanding the suggestion conveyed by the order that
there was urgent business to attend to, the underlying idea is thus
the same as in the summons of 1347 to the Wards, namely to
create a panel of men available for duty whenever called upon.[b]
A meeting was presumably held at once, but we are not told the
nature of the business. The 'bill' must have come as a surprise to
some, for only last year men had been summoned from the Wards
as usual.[6]

Just over a year after this assembly of picked men a meeting
took place in the outer chamber of the Guildhall of which the
record gives an even clearer indication that the gathering was in
essence (if not in name) a true Common Council. It is described as
'a congregation of the Mayor and Aldermen and *men of the
misteries of the City* elected for the business of the Commonalty'.[7]
It is evident from this entry that on this occasion at least the men
from the misteries actually sat with the Mayor and Aldermen as
one elected body. The names of the misteries are unfortunately not
given and we have no clue to their number. But the displacement
of the Wards at this time was in any case of short duration. When
in 1354 we next hear of the Commons being summoned to
Guildhall the customary responsibility for securing the attendance
of members is placed upon the Wards.[8] Nearly twenty-five years
elapse before the issue is again raised in a much more serious and
troublesome form.

In 1352 Old London Bridge comes under our notice with the
election of John de Hatfeld, chandler, as one of the Wardens.[9]
While supreme control was vested in the Corporation of London,
it had long been the practice to commit the care of the bridge to

---

b   Professor Tait observes that as only forty-two representatives in all were elected
from these thirteen 'chief gilds', *in which the Aldermen had a predominant influence*, the
experiment looks more like the work of the ruling oligarchy than of dissatisfied
commoners.[5]

Fig. 17. London Bridge about 1616.

two Bridge Wardens, or 'Masters of the Bridge' as they were often called, who were charged with the collection of the revenues and their disposal in carrying out repairs.[10] Several of the Wardens, including John, held office for ten years or longer. The upkeep of the bridge imposed a heavy burden on the City, and many citizens with pious intent left money and property to be administered by the Bridge Wardens for that purpose. Two other sources of revenue were the rents derived from the letting of shops on the bridge, of which there are said to have been 138 in John de Hatfeld's time,[11] and the rents paid by butchers and fishmongers for their stalls in the Stocks Market set up in the centre of the City by Henry le Waleys in his second term as Mayor (Volume I). The management of this vast trust, for the financial prosperity of which the Wardens were made personally responsible, could be undertaken only by men of the highest standing.

An important feature of the bridge was its chapel founded and endowed by Peter de Colechurch in 1200 in honour of St Thomas the Martyr. Its occupants were the members of a Fraternity of St Thomas known by various titles, including the 'Master and Brethren of the Bridge of London',[12] or the 'Brothers of the Bridge' for short.[13] A number of chantries[c] were established in the chapel, including one in 1334 for our leader, John de Lyndesey,[14] and sixteen years later as many as four chaplains can be seen from the accounts to be officiating in prayers for the souls of benefactors of the bridge.[15] Towards the close of the century yet another chantry was founded when, on the failure of an earlier chantry trust, the Mayor, the then Wardens, 'and Commonalty' came into possession of certain property and rents left by the will of John de Hatfeld *for the maintenance of the bridge and of a chantry in the chapel.*[16]

In 1358 we are again reminded that the City Courts took a serious view of offences committed by makers of candles, whether of tallow or wax. On 31st March three wax-chandlers, on being sworn before the Mayor and Aldermen, pronounced that a certain wax torch in the house of a Lombard was falsely made 'to deceive the people and to the scandal of the whole City'; the torch was forfeited and the culprit committed to prison.[17] In the following June matters were taken a stage further in a civic ordinance prescribing (among other things) that 'torches, cierges, torchyz and priketz should be made of as good wax within as without', and imposing penalties for disobedience, with one important reservation: in supplying torches and the like for private use it was permissible for the maker to mix old wax with new, if asked to do so, provided that the goods were not for sale.[18] (See Riley's translation of this ordinance in Appendix I.)

Four years later we get the earliest of the standard edicts, of which the record has been preserved, regulating the sale of tallow and the manufacture and sale of tallow candles.[19] Its first require-

---

c   Chantry—a service endowed at an altar of a church or chapel by a benefactor for the comfort of his soul or the souls of persons whom he wishes to commemorate.

ment was that chandlers ought to sell a pound of 'candle' for 2*d*. and no more—it will be seen that the price had dropped since Thomas le Chandler's day (Volume I); its second, that butchers ought not to sell 'tallow' to strangers to take out of the City, but should sell it to chandlers of the City; its third, that the price of a wey of 'roughtalwh' should be 18 shillings and a wey of 'moltetalaugh' 22 shillings—from which we conclude that 4 shillings was allowed for rendering. It may seem strange that butchers, although compelled to sell their fat only to tallow chandlers carrying on business *in the City*, should nevertheless be allowed to act as melters, when the buyers, if not performing this task themselves, would certainly have had their own melters within the trade. The explanation may be that in this era—as at other times—the command not to sell to 'strangers' was enforced only when stocks were low. More than a century later we find the City showing more regard for our interests. We read then that butchers were absolutely forbidden to melt any tallow or to make any candles except for their own domestic use.[20]

The final condition of the edict of 1362 was that each wey must contain twenty-eight cloves (clavos) and that the tallow must be weighed by the balance and not by the 'auncer'. The measure known for centuries throughout England as the wey has always varied with different commodities, and the same article has varied in weight in different counties, hence the direction as to content in this order. The history of the wey is bound up with that of the standard pound. It seems that the Roman libra raised to 16 ounces was the commercial pound even before the Norman conquest and that its use in England has never been suspended, notwithstanding the existence of the troy pound and what was known as the tower pound, to say nothing of the series of sexdecimal weights introduced by the early Plantagenets. This pound, known as 'averdepois'[d] (the standard or imperial pound of today), was almost certainly the weight used by our ancestors. We learn from an entry in the City records[22] for 4th June 1519 that in Norfolk 12 stone (= 168 lb) went to the wey of tallow, equivalent to

---

d The best spelling of the word. 'Aver' is an old-established English word for 'goods',[21] and the earlier form 'haberdepase' shows the original pronunciation.

twenty-eight cloves, or nails, of 6 lb each. If 12 stone to the wey was also the measure for London, which seems most likely, then the 'clove' of our Order was a 6-lb clove. The vendors of cheese were welcome to use an 8-lb clove (with thirty-two cloves to the wey), but this was not the clove for us.[e] The following table gives the various measures of weight for tallow according to our reckoning.

$$\left.\begin{array}{l} 14 \text{ lb (i.e. one stone)} \times 12 \\ \text{or } 6 \text{ lb (i.e. one clove or nail)} \times 28 \\ \text{or } 1 \text{ cwt (112 lb)} + \tfrac{1}{2} \text{ cwt (56 lb)} \end{array}\right\} 168 \text{ lb} = 1 \text{ wey}$$

Fig. 18. Edward III averdepois weights of 56, 28 and 14 lb, in the Westgate Museum, Winchester. (From *Historical Metrology*, 1953, by A. E. Berriman.)

The method of weighing prescribed by the Order was in conformity with a statute, known as the 'Statute of Purveyors', passed in 1352[23] making illegal the instrument called 'auncer', 'auncel' or 'auncell',[f] a one-armed single-scaled weighing lever of Asiatic origin. The pivot or fulcrum of this contrivance appears to have been movable and the counterpoise to have been fixed, in

---

e   'Clove—a weight formerly used for wool and cheese... 1619 DALTON, *Countr. Just.* lxv (1630) 149. A weigh of cheese must contain 32 cloues and every cloue 8.1 of averdepois... 1708 KERSEY. Clove is also a Term us'd in Weights: Thus 7 pounds of wooll make a Clove, but in Essex 8 pounds of Cheese and Butter go to the Clove', *O.E.D.*

f   Thought to be the Saxon vernacular utterance of 'lancel' ('lancella' or 'lancelle' in Norman French), diminutive of 'lance', a scale ('lanx', Lat.), which was a word adopted from the Italian, the initial letter 'l' being dropped as if it were the French article.[24]

which respect it resembled the 'Tron' for weighing wool, but its precise construction is not known.[25]

The use of the device known to Londoners as a 'balance' or 'beam' for weighing heavy or 'ponderable' goods, consisting of a pair of scales with a middle pin or pivot, anciently employed in weighing gold and silver, was probably well established in the City as early as the year 1296.[26] The instrument was called the King's Beam or *Great Beam*, to distinguish it from the Small Balance, or Beam, belonging to the Corporation of London, whereby silk and divers other spiceries (speciarie) were weighed.[27] In 1312 the office of weigher of the King's Beam within the City walls was conferred upon a pepperer chosen by a number of misteries, headed by the Pepperers, 'occupying themselves with ponderable goods'[28] which naturally included tallow. The consortium united in the 'forties under the title *mestera averii ponderis*, a body which, in 1345, made a separate Fraternity among themselves, from which developed the Company of Grocers. It was inevitable that these *Grossarii* should be entrusted some twenty years later with the custody and management of the King's Beam.[29] There was a Proclamation in 1382, which one suspects was made at the instigation of this powerful Guild, that no one should buy confections, powders, nor any other 'aver du pois' by any weight used for fine goods, but only by the weight of 'our lord the King', on pain of forfeiture.[30]

The next we hear of this fourteenth-century price-control in the tallow trade is in April 1373, when 'the chandlers and butchers of London' were directed to appear before the Mayor and Aldermen. The tallow chandlers (*candelarii sepi*) received renewed instructions regarding the price at which their candles might be sold and the butchers were again informed what charge they should make for tallow, with the same distinction between the rough kind of tallow and the melted.[31] In December of that year they appeared once more, and on this occasion the butchers were reminded what the raw material was to weigh and how they should weigh it.[32] The object of these orders was evidently to fix the proportion of price between tallow and candle. In eleven years there had been no change in the authorized price of candles. The butchers must, therefore, remain content with 18 shillings a wey for rough fat or 22 shillings for melted tallow.

In 1363—the year following the first of the standard edicts—*Letter-book* G contains a record of monies received by the Chamberlain from 'divers misteries' for a present to the King. Apart from a number of individual subscribers, twenty-seven crafts are represented.[33] The importance of this record to us is the relatively high position occupied by the chandlers with a credit of £8. After taking into account ten of the leading misteries headed by the Mercers, Drapers, Fishmongers and Skinners, each with a contribution of £40, our mistery is top of the list of the remaining seventeen donors, which includes the Ironmongers—later to become one of the Great Twelve Livery Companies—with a donation of £7 18s. 4d., and the Wax-Chandlers with £2. A complete list of the craft subscribers with the respective contributions is given in Appendix J, which also shows the total sum contributed by individuals.

The reason for this act of generosity is not known. The customary need for money to carry out the King's naval and military operations was lacking at the time, for England had not been at war with France since the peace of Bretigny in November 1360. In July 1364 Edward, as we shall see, showed favour to several of the principal subscribers, but the crafts as a whole do not seem to have benefited. In December 1363 the Saddlers of London had gained recognition in a royal grant, which they shared with other cities, boroughs and towns, confirming powers of search for defective work throughout the realm,[34] but the Mistery of Saddlers was not among the major subscribers to the King's present.

The men of another mistery, who were generous contributors, certainly gained nothing. A few months earlier a statute had been passed requiring English merchants in future to deal in only one sort of merchandise, making it quite clear that the King's command was aimed at the *Grocers*, who were said to 'ingross all manner of merchandise vendible' with the object of enhancing the price.[35] Their business methods were probably no better and no worse than those of the other leading misteries, three of whom—the Drapers, Fishmongers and Vintners—seized the opportunity to obtain the Crown's sanction to the exercise of monopolist powers of which they made no secret.

All three charters recited the statute. The grants to the Fishmongers[36] and Vintners[37] forbade any person who was not

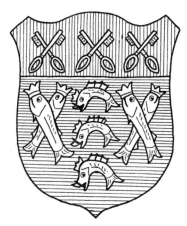

Fig. 19. The Shield of the Worshipful Company of Fishmongers.

enfranchised in their respective misteries to 'meddle' in the trade. The Drapers' grant went further. It precluded anyone from using 'the mistery' (that is to say the trade) who had not actually been apprenticed or received into the trade in some other manner with the assent of the mistery, but, whereas the Fishmongers' and Vintners' grants operated everywhere *within the realm*, the Drapers' grant appears to have been confined to the City of London and suburbs.[38]

The municipal history of London at this period is obscure, although it is clear enough that the charters aroused popular resentment. An immediate rise in prices brought home to the citizens the danger of granting such monopolies.[39] In less than two years the statute was repealed,[40] but we do not know what steps, if any, were taken to curb the unwelcome activities of those who had used it as a pretext for their own advancement.

By this time eight of the principal guilds, counting those whose 'charters' date, as we have seen, from 1327, had been recognized both by the City and the Crown as the acknowledged representatives of their respective crafts, and their wealthier members were doubtless making full use of the exclusive privileges which they now possessed. Because of the jealousy created among the other crafts by the monopoly conferred upon the grantees, these were the powers to attract the most attention. But it must not be overlooked that every one of the eight grants contained, in greater or lesser degree, additional provisions which were highly beneficial to the citizens in general, that is to say the authority to conduct searches for defective goods, the licence to set up standards of quality and workmanship and the right to 'present' offenders for non-compliance therewith, or even for the guild itself to impose penalties. That the Court of Aldermen had a growing appreciation of the need for firm action *in the public interest*, engendered perhaps by the welfare clauses in the charters, and were glad to use the crafts as watchdogs, is seen from their ordinance bearing no date but seeming to belong to the eventful year 1364. It directed that all the misteries of the City should be lawfully ruled and governed, each in its kind, so that no deceit or false work be found by *good men elected and sworn from each mistery*, 'and if any be rebellious against them let him be fined and imprisoned in manner prescribed'.[41] We have an example at this period of particular interest to ourselves of the way in which the Courts studied the needs of the consumer, not only in the maintenance of standards but in safeguarding supplies. We have seen how the stock of tallow was conserved. The case in point is that of John Meredien, butcher, who 'perjured himself' when examined on a charge of having sold a wey of tallow *for conveyance out of the City*, for which he was committed to prison.[42] Yet the prohibition against export was not absolute, as we have already observed. John's case was heard in November 1364. In July 1376 when England was again at war with France the King issued a writ to the Sheriffs to make proclamation forbidding the exportation of various commodities including tallow, *except to Calais*.[43]

To return to the 'sixties. War broke out afresh in April 1369 with a renewal of Edward's claim to the title of King of France.[44] The Letter-book tells us that the City agreed to raise a sum of

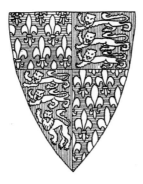

Fig. 20. The Royal Arms 1340–1405.

Edward III, as the son of an heiress of the French Royal Family, was entitled to quarter the fleurs-de-lys with his three lions, placing the French arms in the second and third quarters of the shield. Instead he gave heraldic expression to his claim to the throne of France by setting them in the first and fourth quarters. From *The Romance of Heraldry* by C. W. Scott-Giles (1965), pp. 96–8.

£2,000 for the King, for which purpose an assessment was made in the Wards.[45] On this occasion, we are not given any information regarding the contributors, but among the collectors for Bread Street Ward was a chandler, Robert Lambard.[46] This Robert is on record a few years earlier as one of three 'mainpernors' for a baker's oven-man committed to the prison of Newgate for contempt and trespass against the assayers of white bread. As a condition of his release the three of them undertook, 'body for body', that no damage or peril should befall the assayers at the hands of the culprit or 'by his means'.[47]

In August 1370 a civic ordinance was passed directing for the first time that a daily *watch* should be kept by the *misteries*[48] as distinct from the Wards. The occasion was the presence of 'certain galleys with a multitude of armed men therein, lying off the Foreland of Tenet' (the North Foreland, in the Isle of Thanet), their presumed intention being to come to London 'to destroy the people of that city, and to do other mischief there, if in their power.' The tallow chandlers, as it happens, were not amongst those named for the first and only weekly session, of which details have been preserved, no more than eight of the lesser misteries being mentioned.[49]

The time was rapidly approaching when the crafts' continuous striving after political power would be put to the test. The excuse for a renewed attack on the traditional system under which the members of the Common Council were elected by the Wards came with the impeachment for extortion and other offences of three Aldermen, Richard Lyons, a vintner, Adam de Bury, a skinner and John Peche, a fishmonger, for which the 'Good Parliament', when meeting at the end of April 1376, was responsible.[50]

On 29th July a letter came from the King[51] informing the Mayor and other officers, 'citizens and Commons of the City', that he had heard of dissensions in the City over the elections of Mayor, Sheriffs and Aldermen, and the manner of making ordinances, 'some wishing that such elections and ordinances should be made by certain persons elected by the Wards, whilst others wished them to be made by persons chosen by the Misteries'. It was his purpose to hold a Council at his Palace of Westminster on the Feast of St Michael (29th September) next when the matter could be debated. They were charged meanwhile to put aside all dissension under penalty of forfeiture of their franchise. This was not the first time that the King had intervened in City politics. In January 1366 Adam de Bury had been removed from the office of Mayor by the order of the King—for what reason we do not know[52]—and a new Mayor had been elected in his place.[53] Again, in May 1371 Edward had sent a letter to the Mayor and other officers requiring them to wait

Fig. 21.
Penny of Edward III.   Half-Groat of Edward III.

upon him at Guildhall with 'four of the more sufficient commoners *of each mistery in the City*'.[54] There is more than a suggestion
in this command that the King was looking upon the men of the
misteries as the true 'Commoners'.

The hesitation displayed by the misteries in getting the election
of the Common Council into their hands seems to have been
partly due to the jealousy and distrust existing between the
merchants on the one hand and the handicraftsmen and small
traders on the other. In theory at least all the crafts were now in
favour of the change to mistery rule, but the greater misteries were
alarmed at the prospect of power in the hands of the lesser crafts.
Another disturbing factor was the growing hostility between the
victualling crafts represented by the Grocers, the Fishmongers and
(to a lesser degree) the Vintners and the non-victualling crafts
headed by the Drapers. This uncertainty had already resulted in a
delay of three months in calling a meeting to deprive the delinquent Aldermen of their gowns. The King's letter made action
imperative.

In a matter of hours after the arrival of the letter, the Mayor,
John Warde, with the advice of several Aldermen and Commoners, 'caused the Aldermen and a great number of the Commonalty from *the principal misteries* to be summoned to meet at the
Guildhall on Friday 1st August at 8 o'clock, a "bill" to that effect
being sent under seal to the surveyors of the misteries'.[55] The
reason given for this summons was *the grievous complaint of the
Commonalty of the City* respecting the misdoings 'of which some
persons had been convicted' and the alleged misconduct *for many
years past* 'of divers Mayors and Aldermen'.[g] The meeting was
attended by forty-one crafts, including the 'Talghchandelers',
who are placed twenty-second in the list immediately after the

---

g   See the Introduction to *The History of the Worshipful Company of Drapers of London* by
     the Rev. A. H. Johnson, Vol. I (1914), pp. 28–9, for a discussion as to whether the
     widely held view that John de Northampton, draper, and the non-victualling guilds
     were the chief instigators of this move is correct.

Wax-Chandlers.[h] The first business was to dismiss from office the Aldermen whose delinquencies had thus brought matters to a head. This was followed by a decree that in future the surveyors of *each sufficient mistery* should assemble the men of their mistery to elect certain persons against the day (28th October) when the new Mayor should be sworn and that they should be ready to accept whatever the Mayor, Aldermen and the persons so elected should ordain in the Guildhall. The 'greater misteries' were each required to elect not more than six representatives, and the others four or two according to size. It was resolved that *the persons so elected and no others should be summoned to elections of Mayors and Sheriffs, and whenever it might be necessary to take council of the Commonalty;* further, that if anything should be ordained by the Mayor and Aldermen affecting the Commonalty without the assent of those elected or the greater part of them, *or at least of the twelve principal misteries*, it should be void.[56] The first part of the resolution suggests that this was an attempt to install the same machinery for Mayoral and shrieval elections as for administrative assemblies (which failed), the second that the movement was not quite as democratic as it appears at first sight.[57]

On the same day a reply was sent to the King under the Common Seal of the City[i] denying the existence of any serious dissension, and informing him that whenever the Commonalty met *in Common Council* of the City, the Council should be chosen by the best men of the misteries and not otherwise, *the number of the misteries being regulated by the Mayor according to the gravity of the matter in hand.* The reason given in the letter for these decisions

---

h   The order in which the misteries are placed may have some bearing on their relative importance at this date. Among the first nine are eight of the Great Twelve Livery Companies, together with the Saddlers. They are followed by the Cordwainers and the Girdlers. The Ironmongers (number ten of the 'Great Twelve') are placed twelfth. The Fullers (who, with the Shearmen, later formed the Clothworkers Company—the last of the Twelve) occupy the eighteenth position. Our rivals, the Salters (number nine of the Twelve), are placed immediately after us. The Haberdashers (number eight of the Twelve) are placed twenty-eighth. The Bakers, Barbers, Brewers and Carpenters are notable absentees from the list. By a coincidence, the positions given to the Wax-Chandlers and ourselves are very close to the twentieth and twenty-first places occupied by us today.

i   Mr Johnson points out that among the bearers of this letter were William Walworth and Nicholas Brembre, both of them members of *the Victualling Guilds.*

was 'to prevent tumult arising from large gatherings',[58] an explanation which the King was prepared to accept, 'provided no further cause were given for complaint.'[59]

Fig. 22. Edward III—from the tomb at Westminster Abbey.

The City under mistery rule

IT took little more than a week to put the new plan into operation. On Saturday 9th August (1376) 'an immense Commonalty' from fifty-one[a] misteries came to the Guildhall and presented the names of those elected by each mistery and 'deputed to serve as a Council for the City until the charge (*oneratio*) of a new Mayor.'[1] Only *eight* of the fifty-one crafts ranked at that time as 'greater misteries'. Each sent six representatives, as directed. They were the Mercers, Grocers, Drapers, Fishmongers, Goldsmiths, Skinners, Tailors and Vintners, all members of the Great Twelve Livery Companies of today. The Haberdashers, Salters

Fig. 23. The Shields of the Worshipful Companies of Skinners and Merchant Taylors.

---

a   The number is usually given as forty-seven. The difference is accounted for by the fact that five separate crafts, the Loriners, Farriers, Bladesmiths, Blacksmiths and Heumers (makers of helmets), are listed together as 'smiths'. The Bakers and Brewers (omitted from the earlier list) are now included. The Barbers and Carpenters are again omitted.

J.Schnebbelie, del. 1788.

G.Hollis, sculp.

OLD FRONT OF THE GUILDHALL, LONDON.

Plate IV. By the courtesy of the Guildhall Library, London.

and Ironmongers had yet to find a place among 'the Twelve'. The Clothworkers were a later incorporation of the Fullers and Shearmen. Ten crafts, including the Ironmongers and Fullers, each sent four men to the meeting. For some unknown reason our rivals (the Salters), the Butchers and we ourselves, sent only three. Of the remaining thirty misteries, twenty-six, including the Haberdashers, Leathersellers and Wax-Chandlers, sent two. Four crafts were content with one representative each. All those present 'were called separately for each mistery' and bound themselves to give good and lawful counsel 'according to their understanding and knowledge', not to claim any individual benefit against the common weal of the City, and to preserve for each mistery 'its reasonable customs'.

The Tallow Chandlers are given the name of Chandelers de Su[if][b] in this list, an apt description which occurs again in our grant of arms eighty years later. Our representatives were Richard Willesdone, John Goldryng and Richard Manhale. The first Richard, with Agnes his wife, owned several shops in the parish of St Christopher, near the Stocks, purchased a few years earlier[2] from Geoffrey, the youngest son of John de Westwyk, whom we met in the 'thirties. Richard (the purchaser) is seen on his death in 1398 to have been the owner of other City properties, situated in Lothbury, Mincing Lane and Tower Street.[3] For John's property interests we must turn to his will dated 29th December 1397, directing that his 'lands and tenements' in Distaff Lane in the old parish of St Margaret Moses (later united to St Mildred, Bread Street) should be sold, and that part of the proceeds should be devoted to the relief of prisoners in Newgate and Ludgate.[4] The second Richard, alias Richard Stondon, called 'Manhale', with his wife Cecilia, owned a 'tenement' in the parish of St Peter, Cornhill, purchased in 1373.[5] This Richard's relationship to the earlier Manhales is not known. We shall be meeting these three men again.

On 12th March (1377) a bill was sent to 'the more powerful misteries', numbering—according to the record—fifty-one, to the

---

b   Fr. Suet, tallow.

effect that they should cause the masters, servants, apprentices and all others of their mistery to swear that they would maintain the King's peace, readily obey the summons of the Mayor, Aldermen and other ministers of the City, put down conspiracies, keep secret the City's counsel and attend at the Guildhall only if elected by the misteries, or summoned, or 'when compelled by their own necessities'.[6] The names of the crafts are not given. The number 'fifty-one' suggests that the same misteries attended on this occasion as were present at the August Assembly, but this is not necessarily so, for there was another meeting later on when a list of fifty-one misteries is given which contains several new names.[7]

Earlier that August two Aldermen and six Commoners, all members of the greater misteries, constituting in fact, if not in name, a citizen committee, were elected to survey and examine the ordinances reposing in the Guildhall and to present to the Commonalty those that were of benefit to the City and those that were not.[8] Among the articles granted by Edward II in 1319 had been one to the effect that the Aldermen of the City should be 'removable' every year on the Feast of St Gregory [12th March]. There was grave doubt as to whether the ordinance was merely permissive or whether compulsory removal was intended and for that reason it appears to have remained a dead letter. That an Alderman in London held a unique position of authority is evident. Not only did he preside over the ward-mote, which met to enquire into breaches of the peace, the commission of nuisances and many other matters, but it was also his duty to attend in person to the enforcement of the regulations and to see to the punishment of offenders.[9] His standing in the City at this period is well illustrated by the orders given on the death of Edward III in June 1377 for safeguarding the City, when the French were threatening the south coast. Each Alderman was commanded 'to put his Ward into array under his pennon[c] *bearing his arms in relief*, and to lead

---

c   The pennon was the personal ensign of the knight (or, in this case, the Alderman) who bore it. It was small, pointed or swallow-tailed at the fly and was borne immediately below the lance-head. It was 'charged' with the badge or other armorial device of the bearer and sometimes was richly fringed with gold.[10]

his men withersoever commanded for the defence of the City.'[11]
The committee of eight, with facts such as these in mind, may
well have been responsible for getting the meaning of the
ordinance made clear, as we shall see was the case, by a royal
charter dated 22nd November 1376.[12]

Fig. 24. The Crests of the Worshipful Companies of Haberdashers,
Ironmongers and Clothworkers.

On 6th March 1377 the Mayor and Aldermen with sixty-four
chosen men of thirteen misteries assembled 'as a Council in the
Chamber of the Guildhall'. We do not know their names, but we
do know that four of our men attended this decisive meeting.[13]
There were present six representatives from seven of the greater
misteries, four from five of the lesser crafts, including ourselves, and
two from one other.[d] The Council issued an order that anyone who
had been an Alderman and who, 'for reasonable and true cause and
for his own faults and demerits', had been removed from office,
should on no account be re-elected either then or at some future date.
The meeting declared that the intention of the old ordinance (as
the new Charter explained) was that *all* the Aldermen should
cease to hold office on St Gregory's day in each year and should
not be re-elected, but it gave a conservative interpretation to this

---

[d]   The reader will see that we had our full complement on this occasion. Among those
also sending four representatives were the Haberdashers, of whom only two attended
the meeting on 9th August. The Armourers were again represented by two members.

provision, namely that those who had borne themselves well and had gone out of office *without any evidence of their having misbehaved themselves* might, after their successors had served their year, be re-elected. On St Gregory's day next—less than a week later—the good men of the Wards met and elected their Aldermen,[14] and a year later there was a complete change.[15] The new arrangement continued without a break for another six years, but in 1384 an irregularity occurred which caused the Mayor 'and Commonalty' to petition the King to confirm the election, to which he agreed.[16] After this no serious attempt was made to enforce the rule that Aldermen might not stand for election in successive years, and ten years later the formality of re-election was abolished by statute.[17]

The dispute between the victualling and non-victualling crafts which split the City into two camps owed its origin to the victuallers' struggle to secure for themselves a trade monopoly in consumer goods, a struggle which became of national importance due to the victuallers, led by Nicholas Brembre, a grocer, throwing in their lot with the young King, and their opponents, under the leadership of John de Northampton, a draper, supporting Richard's uncle, John of Gaunt, Duke of Lancaster. The cry of the non-victuallers was that, due to their monopoly, the fishmongers in particular were raising the price of the people's food. The victuallers, on the other hand, declared that the trading privileges of the Londoners were being threatened by foreign merchants and that their freedom was being attacked by the Duke.[e]

The leading merchants thus had a two-fold problem; it was their ambition to maintain an over-all majority in the Common Council by excluding as many voters from the lesser misteries as possible, and at the same time to secure control of the Council by whichever political group they favoured as the party most likely to further their interests.

---

e   A good idea of the intense rivalry between the two factions can be obtained from Dr Sharpe's diary of events in the Introduction to his *Calendar of Letter-book H*, pp. xxxiii–xliv, where he also relates the successive steps taken to bring Northampton under control.

One of the last acts of Edward III had been to forbid 'strangers', that is to say non-freemen, to sell goods to other strangers within the City to be sold again,[f] until the question had been settled by Parliament, and by Letters Patent of 4th December 1376 strangers had been absolutely forbidden to sell merchandise in the City by retail[18] 'saving unto the merchants of the House of Almaine their ancient liberties'.[g] At the crucial election of new Aldermen on 12th March 1377 twelve were victuallers and eleven, including a wax-chandler, Roger Elys—one of the very few men elected from the lesser misteries—belonged to the other party. The Mayor, Adam Stable, was a mercer. The opposing parties *on the Court* were, therefore, equal.[h] A few days later, as a conciliatory gesture to the Duke of Lancaster, who had suffered an indignity at the hands of the London mob,[19] Stable was removed from office by King Edward, then suffering from his last illness, and on 21st March Brembre was elected in his place.[20] In October he was re-elected[21] and less than two months afterwards the new King confirmed his grandfather's Charter.[22] Brembre had the new Charter publicly proclaimed[23] and in April (1378) sent a precept to eight of the greater misteries[i] to conduct searches for merchant strangers bringing merchandise to the City.[24] But six months later, by the action of Parliament, the Charter was annulled and non-freemen were again given the right to sell both in gross and by retail.[25]

Notwithstanding this set-back, the principal victuallers, having a majority on the Court of Aldermen, ruled the City for four years. They were, however, in a minority on the Common Council, even when supported by the lesser victuallers such as the Bakers, the Brewers and the Poulterers. So far as is known the

---

f The right of lords of the realm 'and all others' to buy merchandise for their own use in gross, that is to say, *wholesale*, was expressly preserved.

g The merchants of Almaine, frequently referred to in London records, belonged to the Hanse, a society established *c*. 1140 as the Hanseatic League for the purpose of trade.

h The Wards of that time numbered twenty-four, of which Portsoken was one. The Prior of Christ Church, or Holy Trinity, Aldgate, being *ex officio* the Alderman of that Ward, did not take part in the election.

i The Ironmongers are named on this occasion to the exclusion of the Tailors.

Tallow Chandlers took no part in these disputes. They were well represented on the Council, as we have seen, but which side they favoured, if any, we cannot say. There is no reason to suppose that their domestic trade in candles was being threatened by foreign competition. They would thus have derived no particular benefit from siding with the victuallers. They are more likely to have been followers of John de Northampton, who posed as the champion of the lesser crafts. But when the Mercers later complained to Parliament that both Brembre's elections in the 'eighties had been carried by display of force and not by free election[26] we did not follow the Cordwainers in supporting them, as did eight other crafts.[j]

That the new system of electing Commoners entirely from the misteries had its opponents is seen from the record in the Letter-book of 'a Common Council' in November 1379, when there were present the Mayor, the Aldermen and good men chosen from the several misteries, *as well as others of the more powerful and discreet citizens.*[27] Again, in October of the following year, there is a record of a 'congregation' of the Mayor, Aldermen and Commoners elected by each mistery, *as well as by the Wards* for a Common Council of the City.[28] It is highly probable that the victuallers were mainly responsible for these mixed assemblies. We are told that in November (1380) the Aldermen received a precept (from the Mayor) to summon the inhabitants of their Wards to consider whether it were better for the Common Council to be elected from the misteries 'as heretofore' or from the best men of the Wards, or partly from the misteries and partly from the Wards.[29] The result of the meeting, if held, is not on record, but there seems little doubt that further action by Brembre's party to restore the Wards to their traditional position was arrested only by the return of the non-victuallers to power through Northampton's capture of the Mayoralty in October 1381.[30]

---

j   They were the Founders, Saddlers, Painters, Armourers, Embroiderers, Spurriers, Bladesmiths and Pinners. Bishop Stubbs inadvertently omits the last-named mistery in his *Constitutional History of England* (Volume III, p. 621).

Fig. 25. John of Gaunt.

Northampton retained office for two years and, during that period, the rights of foreign victuallers were confirmed,[31] but at the election in October 1383 his opponent, Brembre, again became Mayor,[32] and was re-elected in each of the two following years.[33] He soon secured the repeal of the foreigners' statute[34] and the citizens' trade monopoly was restored.[k] He next turned his attention as Mayor to the vexed question of mistery control, in which undertaking he probably had the support by now of most other merchants. It is recorded that on Friday 29th January 1384— a few days before Northampton's arrest on suspicion of planning an insurrection in the City[35]—in the presence of the Mayor, Aldermen and an immense Commonalty of 'honest and discreet men of the City in the Guildhall assembled' certain [draft]

k   The monopoly was again lost in 1388 when 'the Merciless Parliament' declared free trade throughout England. In May 1389 Richard, in an attempt to gain the support of the victuallers, confirmed the privileges of the Fishmongers.

ordinances were put forward for consideration. There had been a preliminary meeting—summoned, one suspects, by the wealthier merchants—'to consider how matters in the Common Council had been carried *by clamour rather than by reason*', and sometimes by 'members' who were not qualified to act, whereby tumults had arisen. There were two suggestions. First, in order that the Common Council might be composed of 'men qualified by reason and understanding', the Aldermen should, no later than fifteen days after their election, *assemble their Wards* and charge them to elect certain qualified persons (regardless of any office they might have held before) to be of a Common Council for the year ensuing,[1] with the important proviso that not more than eight persons in all of the same mistery were to be accepted. Secondly, the number from each Ward was to be proportionate to the number of the inhabitants, with a maximum of six.[36]

The reactionaries won the day. At a Common Council later that same eventful Friday, an ordinance was made that the Council should in future be held by men of the *Wards*, instead of by men of the misteries 'as recently ordained'.[37]

The acceptance of this new decree was confirmed on 31st July (1384) at a congregation of the Mayor, Aldermen and 'good and sufficient men summoned from the Wards' as a Common Council.[38] The effect of returning to the old system had been to re-establish merchant majorities.[m] It should not surprise us, therefore, to read that in the autumn (or winter) of 1385 the ordinance was reaffirmed at a Council meeting which found that on trial it had proved to be convenient and advantageous, and declared that it 'should continue for ever'.[39] The victory was a severe blow to the lesser crafts from which they never recovered.

The task of electing a certain number of men from each Ward

The number proposed for each Ward was four, but this was inconsistent with the second suggestion and the proposal was evidently overruled.

m   See the Table prepared by Miss Sylvia Thrupp, p. 80 of *The Merchant Class of Medieval London* (1948). Her analysis shows that those identified as members of merchant companies returned at the election of July 1384 numbered 169, while those of other companies numbered 82, compared with 57 and 96 respectively at the election on 9th August 1376.

according to its size *without respect of their particular mistery* was assigned to the Mayor in the presence of twelve Aldermen in 1389[40] but, twenty years later, when we next hear of a Common Council being summoned, the duty of electing Commoners is again seen to be in the hands of the Aldermen of the Wards.[41]

These decrees applied only to meetings of the Common Council, that is to say to administrative assemblies. Electoral assemblies continued for a time to be 'managed' much as before. A proclamation made in October 1384 on the eve of Nicholas Brembre's election as Mayor for the third time affords a good example. In future no one was to attend elections in the City except the Mayor, Aldermen and good folk elected by the Wards to serve as a Common Council *and others who should be summoned from the Wards* by the advice of the said Mayor and Aldermen, on pain of imprisonment, forfeiture of goods and loss of franchise.[42] In 1443 *'those who were of the Common Council of the City'* were specially summoned *'with certain other powerful and discreet citizens from the several Wards'* for the election of the Mayor.[43] In 1467 there is a record in the Letter-book of an ordinance of the Common Council that thenceforth the election of Mayor and Sheriffs shall be made 'only by the Common Council, *the Masters of each Mistery of the City*, coming in their Livery, and by other good men specially summoned for the purpose.'[44] Nevertheless, in referring to the persons actually summoned, the stock phrase for shrieval elections continues to be 'very many Commoners', and for Mayoral elections 'an immense commonalty', and no further mention is made of the Common Council itself as the electoral body. In 1475 it was agreed at a meeting of the Common Council 'that the *Masters and Wardens of the Misteries*, together with good men of the same, assembled in their halls or other convenient places, should proceed together to the Guildhall, *clothed in their last livery* for the election of a Mayor, and in their previous livery for the election of Sheriffs: also that no others except good men of the Common Council should be present at such elections'.[45] In requiring the men of the misteries to assemble at their halls or elsewhere before proceeding to vote, the Council was doubtless confirming an established practice dating from the ordinance of

1467, or earlier. In stipulating that those attending Common Hall should not be newly clothed for the election of the Sheriffs, it was probably re-enacting an order which, as we shall see, had been made in 1389.

Thus, there was substituted for an ill-defined muster of commoners a definite class of voters of recognized standing, namely the liverymen of the City Guilds or Livery Companies as they were later to be known, an electorate quite different from the customary body charged with the election of the Common Council.[n]

The names of individuals attending Council meetings during the time that the City was under mistery rule are rarely given, but an instance occurs in the Mayoralty of John de Northampton (1381–2), when representatives of forty-nine misteries attended. We had our full complement of four, headed by our old friend Richard Manhale. The others were Robert Kyng, John Brokholl and Richard Breyngwayn (or Brangwayn).[47]

The mention of Richard Brangwayn is a reminder that only a few years earlier, during Nicholas Brembre's first term as Mayor —on 26th September 1377 to be precise—we find the first recorded case of four 'Masters' of our Mistery being sworn before the Mayor and Aldermen, together with the Masters of other misteries, including, as it happens, those of the Wax-Chandlers of whom (at that time) there were two.[48] This important subject remains to be dealt with in a later chapter.

Richard was the second-named of our four Masters at this time, the others being William atte Lee, alias William Brynehelle (see Appendix L, note a), John Hockele (or Hockeley) and Thomas Frankeleyn (or Fraunkleyn). Richard and William were two of the many commoners summoned for the Council meeting of 31st July 1384, the former as a representative for the Ward of

---

n   The exclusive electoral rights of the Liverymen of the Companies in the assembly now known as 'the Liverymen in Common Hall assembled' were affirmed by Statute in 1725.[46] On Midsummer Day they elect the Sheriffs and at Michaelmas they nominate for Lord Mayor two Aldermen who have served as Sheriffs for presentation to the Court of Aldermen, which body makes the final selection.

Bridge,[49] and the latter for Tower Ward.[50] William—a property owner in two parishes[51]—was a subscriber, as were other chandlers, to a loan to the City in 1379 for payment to those 'lords of the realm' who had withdrawn themselves from London, to induce them to return. We are told that, due to this expenditure and by the diligence and work of certain good folk of the City, a good accord was effected between the lords and the City, 'thanks be to God!'[52]

Nothing seems to be known of John Hockele's public life; he was not a subscriber to the loan to the City in 1379, but it appears from the *Husting Rolls* that he was a rich man. We learn from a

Fig. 26. Female dress, time of Richard II (Royal MS. 16 Gv, and Harleian MS. 4379).

deed of the year 1380 that he and his wife were the owners of property, not only in London and Southwark, but also in the counties of Kent and Essex[53] formerly belonging to William Hatfeld (or de Hatfeld).[o] Thomas Frankeleyn was one of three

---

o   The owner at his death in 1369 of shops in Oynters' Row, West Chepe (see sections K and L of the Guide in Volume I and supra).

collectors appointed in 1373 of the sum of 12*d*. levied on every boat coming to the City with rushes, the money to be expended on cleansing the ports, quays, etc. of the City where such boats discharged.[54] He was a property owner in the City[55] and, as we shall see, he had the distinction of serving a second time as one of our Masters in 1393.[56]

Of the other two commoners elected from our Mistery to serve with Richard Manhale and Richard Brangwayn on the Common Council in Northampton's mayoralty, Robert Kyng was evidently one of our senior members at that time, for, in July 1388, he was discharged by the Mayor and other officers from serving on juries and the like 'owing to increasing old age'.[57] He was at one period the owner of a shop in Gracechurch Street[58] where he had as a neighbour our John de Hatfeld (Warden of London

Fig. 27. Hogarth's view of the houses on London Bridge removed in 1760 after having been twice rebuilt, first in 1633 when a fire destroyed those on the northern end and again after the Great Fire of 1666. The bridge itself stood for over 600 years until taken down and replaced by the bridge known to Londoners for the past 140 years, which in turn must make way for a brand-new bridge containing dual three-lane carriage-ways to handle modern traffic.

Bridge), by whose will he was given the custody of John's infant daughter Dionisia.[59] Nothing is known of John Brokholl beyond the fact that in 1406 he was a joint beneficiary of property in the parish of St John upon Walbrook under the will of Robert Lodewyk,[60] another of our Masters, whom we have yet to meet.

At an earlier meeting (in November 1378) of persons elected by the Common Council to sit as a Committee with the Mayor and Aldermen[61] we find the name of Thomas Mordone, chandler,[p] among thirteen commoners, of whom nine[q] were representatives of the greater misteries and four[r] came from the lesser crafts. Thomas was a subscriber to the City loan of 1379.[62] On his death in 1386 he owned a house in Wood Street,[63] but some thirteen years earlier he appears to have been living 'near to Billingsgate' where he had one John Lithfot (or Lightfoot) *salter* residing with him.[64] We shall meet Thomas later as a Commoner of the Ward of Billingsgate after the restoration of Common Council elections to the Wards.

The City was still under the rule of the misteries when, on 6th December 1383, we learn of the first of two searches conducted by Vintners on both sides of the Walbrook, the party on each occasion being accompanied by one chandler—John Goldryng (our Commoner of the 'seventies)—who went with the Vintners 'of the West part' and Richard Manhale, who went with those 'of the East part'. The searchers were sworn for the scrutiny of wines in cellars and other places where wines were sold, and to pour out into the 'kennel' (or gutter) all such wines as were found unhealthy and corrupt, to prevent old wines from being stored with new, and '*together with the Chandlers*' to survey vinegar and sauces kept in the shops and cellars of chandlers and to pour away such as were condemned.[65] It appears from the order that our two named representatives had the duty of summoning other chandlers

---

p   Alias Mordon or de Mordon. Surely a different person from Thomas de Mordon, found guilty in 1354 of forestalling the market in salt (see page 47).

q   Mercers, Grocers, Drapers, Fishmongers, Skinners, Vintners, Goldsmiths, Tailors and Ironmongers.

     Cordwainers, Armourers, Chandlers and Saddlers.

to accompany the search parties on the first occasion but not so in the following November. On this second search the parties were required to give a certificate to the Mayor and Aldermen as to how much old red and white wine there was in each place and to see that the vinegar and *other* sauces of the chandlers were sound.[66]

Fig. 28. Male costume, time of Richard II (Royal MS. 20 B vi, and Harleian MS. 1319).

The aftermath

WITH the return of Common Council elections to the Wards come detailed lists of the Commoners attending.

The men of our Mistery present as Ward representatives on 31st July 1384 were Richard Brangwayn (Tower), Thomas Mordone (Billingsgate), Richard Manhale (Cornhill), John Sandhurst and William atte Lee (Bridge), Gilbert Mersshe (Vintry), Richard Willesdone (Broad Street), John Goldryng (Bread Street) and Thomas Chaundeler (Queenhithe). Only John Sandhurst, or Sandherst, Gilbert Mersshe, or atte Mersshe (see Appendix L, note *a*) and Thomas Chaundeler are new names to us. John's will affords ample proof that he was a rich man with 'lands, tenements and rents' in three London parishes.[1] The evidence of the *Husting Rolls* of Gilbert's property interests in the City is equally impressive.[2] Of Thomas Chaundeler we know nothing, beyond the fact that he later became a resident of another Ward where he caught the eye of the Serjeant of the Chamber when jurors were required to settle a boundary dispute.[3] Except for Thomas Mordone, of whom we do not hear again, all those attending on 31st July were present as Commoners at the election of Nicholas Brembre as Mayor on 13th October, with the addition of John Cook (or Cok), who accompanied Richard Manhale as a Ward representative for Cornhill.[4] John had property in the parish of St Michael Cornhill,[5] but resided in the adjoining parish of St Peter, where he evidently carried on his trade as a chandler dealing in *vinegar*, for on his death a few years later he left one of his colleagues all his vessels with vinegar (*cum vino agro*) lying in his *house* except for one jar which he bequeathed 'to the use of' Isabella, his wife.[6] While on the subject of vinegar, we may note the will of Thomas de Felmyngham, chandler, dated 6th June 1368, leaving his wife a life interest in part of his stock in trade with the remainder to his four apprentices.[7] In addition to broches, or broaches (Volume I), and candle moulds, his goods consisted of *molas pro salseis factis et non factis* as well as jars (*dolea*) for vinegar. *Mola* may signify a measure[a] or (in this context) more probably a *mill*, used for grinding mustard or other substances in the making of sauces.

All those attending the meeting on 13th October 1384, with the exception of John Sandhurst, are recorded as having been present at the Common Council 'of the eighth year of Richard II (1384–5)' with the addition of Thomas Frankeleyn, accompanying Thomas Chaundeler for Queenhithe.[8]

Three of our 'regulars'—Richard Manhale, John Sandhurst and Richard Willesdone—with Thomas Frankeleyn and one John Chaundeler (Cornhill), who is not mentioned again—were among those elected at a meeting in the Council Chamber of the Guildhall on 18th July 1385 to take steps for safeguarding the realm. The occasion was the threatened descent on England of 'a great number of ships of France and Flanders in the absence of the King

Fig. 29. Ships of the time of Richard II (Harl. MS. 1319).

---

a   As rendered by Dr Sharpe in his *Calendar of Wills*.

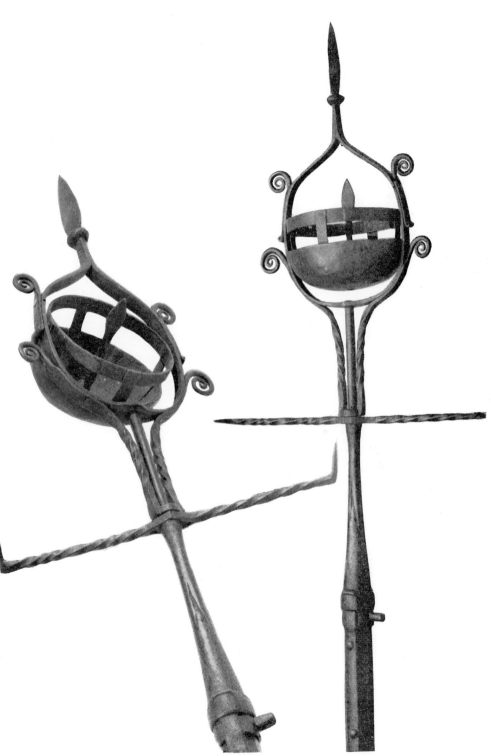

Plate V. Early eighteenth-century cresset with hemispherical bowl and central spike for securing a ball of combustible material (Tower of London). Crown Copyright.

on the borders of Scotland'. The means adopted by the meeting for dealing with the menace was the usual one of a levy upon the inhabitants, those who were not freemen, and on that account not sharing in the City's charges, being called upon this time to pay double.[9] Attendances at later Council meetings, together with those already mentioned, are given in the Table in Appendix K. It will be seen that the only new name is that of Roger Haukewelle who appears from the *Husting Roll* to have had a shop in Old Fish Street.[10] William atte Lee attended on 25th March 1386 notwithstanding that he had only recently been discharged by the Mayor and Aldermen from serving on assizes, juries, etc., 'owing to increasing old age'.[11] Roger Haukewelle, discharged 'for like cause' in the following June, was still alive twelve years later.[12] John Goldryng, on the other hand, died within three years of his discharge.[13]

Among the less dramatic events of this turbulent reign several matters of general interest and some of special concern to tallow chandlers remain to be mentioned.

There was a proclamation in June 1378[14] that everyone of estate (*chescun homme destat*) should keep a barrel or 'tyne' of water before his house by day and night[b] 'on account of the dryness of the season in case of sudden fire'.

In the same month a letter was sent to the Aldermen with directions for setting the Watch on the eves of the Nativity of St John the Baptist (24th June) and St Peter and St Paul (29th June). Each Alderman and the good men of his Ward were to be 'well and sufficiently armed', and arrayed in red and white,[c] particoloured, *over their armour*.[16] Seven years later the Aldermen were arrayed entirely in red. The clothing of their retinues 'and other good folks' would have been seen by spectators as a 'field'[d] of white,[17] to which they would have witnessed in the following

---

b   The idea was evidently not a new one, for when the order was repeated in the following year the words 'according to custom' were added.[15]

c   The City colours—just as they are today.

d   The heraldic term for the surface of the shield (normally) on which arms are depicted.

year (1386) the addition of a 'bend'[e] of red.[18] The Watch in 1378 was to be kept 'in manner as done heretofore, for the honour of the City, and for keeping the peace'. The procession was to pass through the City with 'cressets', the men of each Ward having 'lances' (meaning the flags or pennons attached thereto) of different colours, some 'powdered' with stars or, as the heralds would say, 'semé d'estoiles'. The cresset was a metal vessel (mounted on a pole) usually made of wrought iron, which might be in the form of a bowl to hold grease or oil, or a bowl (or basket) with a central spike to take some combustible material such as pitched rope (see Plate V) or a basket or grated fire pan to take coal. In a precept of 1384 the number of lighted cressets prescribed for each Ward was two.[19] In the orders issued to the Aldermen in 1386 the command

Fig. 30. The Marching Watch.

---

e   The figure or 'charge' formed by two diagonal lines, sometimes erroneously referred to as a bar.

was for 'two cressets at least, or more, if you may'. A precept of 1379 specified '*four* iron cressets burning',[20] but this may have been a special occasion. It became the business of the Livery Companies later to furnish these lights, and it seems probable that the practice was of long standing.

From the precept of 1379 and from that of the following year[21] we learn what armour was considered suitable for the men of the Watch. A 'basynet' or 'bassynet' (a light steel head-piece), gauntlets of plates, and a hatchet or axe are mentioned as a necessary part of their equipment in both orders, to which a harbergeon (a sleeveless coat or jacket of mail), a sword and a dagger are added in the second, all 'according to their estate'. 'Inferior men' were to be arrayed with bows and arrows as well as 'sword and buckler', weapons with which the reader is already familiar.

The correct garb for Aldermen when performing their official duties was also specified at this period. On the occasion of the Mayoral election in 1378 each Alderman was commanded to ride 'in honour of the City' with the Mayor from the Guildhall to Westminster arrayed in cloak and hood at least, particoloured with red, scarlet and white, 'the red on the right side'.[22] In 1381 an Alderman was sentenced to provide a dinner for the Mayor as the penalty for appearing in a cloak without a lining.[23] Eight years later it became necessary, however, to curb what was then considered unnecessary expenditure on the part of 'divers misteries' in the matter of 'vesture' and the hire of horses. It had been the custom for their men to be arrayed in *a new suit* and to hire horses and incur other expenses at the presentation of the Sheriffs before the Barons of the Exchequer on the morrow of St Michael [29 September] and, when the Mayor rode to Westminster on the morrow of SS. Simon and Jude [28 October], to incur similar expenses. On the occasion of the election of William Venour, grocer, as Mayor in October 1389—an election which incidentally was hotly contested by those in the opposite camp[24]—it was accordingly decided that in future the Sheriffs should give clothing only to the City's officers and their own serjeants, and that they should no longer ride, but should go to Westminster by water or on foot, and that those of the misteries who were willing to accompany them *should go in their last clothing and not have new clothing given to them*, under penalty of 100 marks to the Chamber.[25]

The behaviour of those who walked the streets by night was carefully observed as heretofore. The wearing of visors or masks, false faces 'or other strange guise', whereby the owner's identity might be concealed was strictly forbidden.[26] Apart from such activities as these, the carrying of arms was unlawful except by a peer of the realm or a knight or his valet, or an esquire of the King's household, or some lord. A knight must be content with one sword and an esquire or valet was permitted to carry his lord's or master's sword only *in his presence*.[27] The King's writ of October 1384 directed to the Mayor, prohibiting anyone at all to go armed at that time, is referred to later in this chapter. In 1389 there was a general proclamation forbidding night-walking of any kind after curfew.[28] In December 1391, when the peace of the realm appeared to have been restored,[29] the bearing of arms was again allowed to certain privileged persons,[30] but withdrawn two years later because of disturbances by armed bands.[31]

In March 1381 it was decided by the Common Council that, in certain cases, the fee for admission to the freedom of the City was too high, resulting in poor persons withdrawing to Southwark or Westminster, and many houses in the City on that account standing empty. It was, accordingly, ordained 'at a full meeting' that the Chamberlain, associated with two Aldermen, might in future admit any fit or proper person to the freedom by redemption 'for a sum suitable to his estate'.[32] The rule introduced in the reign of Edward II, that an applicant following a trade might be admitted only on the security of six honest and sufficient men of the mistery which he followed, was still in force. It was re-enacted at a Council meeting in June 1384, with the addition of an order that the applicant should be received in the presence of an Alderman and the Chamberlain 'paying more or less according to his estate and as the six men aforesaid might testify concerning his ability to pay.'[33]

These two ordinances were doubtless responsible for a number of cases in which an applicant for the freedom carrying on a

Fig. 31. Gold Noble of Richard II.

certain specified trade had, as his sponsors, men of a different trade, who, if not actually in league with him, had certainly taken no trouble to ascertain his true circumstances; and the sad fact is that some men (unnamed) of our Mistery were, as we shall see, involved in one of them.

A few months after the second ordinance two applicants each using the 'art' of mercery were received into the freedom of Haberdashers 'as if using the mistery of haberdasherie'. It was given in evidence that the fee paid by one of the applicants was 20 shillings, 'whereas if he had been enfranchised by good folk of the Mercers, *who knew him and whose mistery he used*, he would not have been admitted to the franchise without payment of *a large sum*'. The other applicant, also paying 20 shillings, confessed that he had obtained the franchise by deceit being able to pay as much as £40. Both freedoms were annulled.[34] Other cases reported at this time concerned an applicant who was using 'the art of Drapers' posing as a weaver and another draper posing as a tailor. Both freedoms were annulled, and the sureties were condemned to lose their franchise.[35]

In 1395 two broderers (or embroiderers), confessing that they had been admitted 'into the Mistery of Tailors' through ignorance of the custom of the City, prayed that they might be admitted into the Mistery of Broderers. Compared with previous sentences, the decision in their case was a lenient one. It seems that they were readmitted to the freedom of the City 'by surety of good men of the Mistery of Broderers', on payment of a fine of £3 each.[36] In the case with which we were concerned three years later the culprit fared even better. One William Livegood had been admitted to the freedom of the City in the Mistery of 'Chaundellers', whilst he was using only the mistery of Vintners and *was yearly clad with the livery of that mistery*. He had never (so it was said) had any communication with our Mistery, which, if true, disposes of the theory that he might have been associated with us in one of the joint searches for vinegar. His prayer that he might be admitted to the freedom of the City as a vintner was granted 'at the instance of good men of the Mistery of Vintners'. He paid for his admission 40 shillings, nothing being said about a fine.[37] If the six members of our Mistery who, one would think, must have sponsored his first application suffered any penalty, it is not recorded.

For a time freedom by redemption appears to have fallen into disrepute. In 1408 a petition by the Commonalty that the freedom of the City might thenceforth be obtained *by apprenticeship only* was approved at a meeting of the Common Council,[38] and in December 1434 the Aldermen were directed that only freemen by birth or apprenticeship, *and not by redemption*, should be elected as members of the Common Council,[39] but neither order seems to have been taken very seriously. The only way in which fraudulent admissions to the freedom could be curbed was by continuing to disfranchise the culprits when their offence became known. How effective (if at all) was a decree made in February 1433 that no one should be admitted to the freedom by redemption in any fellowship without a guarantee that such admission was not prejudicial to another fellowship[40] we do not know. Irregular admissions continued to take place and 'translation' from one mistery to another— or 'changing of copie'—became commonplace. Sometimes the translation came about through a man who had been admitted in a company *by patrimony* taking up a different trade from that of his father. At other times a man might genuinely desire to change his occupation, an eventuality for which express provision had been made in 1365.*f* Later we shall witness two translations of practising tallow chandlers to our own Company[42] with no imputation of fraud in either case, yet both men had, on their own admission, long been using a trade other than the nominal trade of their mistery. Much later (in 1675) the translation took place from our Company to the Drapers of one of our benefactors, Sir Joseph Sheldon, in anticipation of the Mayoralty, to which anciently only members of *the Great Twelve Livery Companies* could aspire.[43]

In July 1387 attention of a different kind was drawn to freedom admissions. It was agreed then that those claiming the freedom by patrimony must take the same oath as other applicants.[44] It may seem strange that such a rule should not have been made before, but it must not be forgotten that freedom by inheritance was the original, basic form of citizenship, and that the other freedoms, well-established customs as they had become by now, had arisen by a process of evolution. This ordinance was proclaimed in the following month accompanied by an order directed to freemen living *outside the City*, whose status as citizens had been preserved by an ordinance passed in 1365 to the effect that they should not lose their freedom provided they were 'in scot and lot'.[45] Such persons 'using merchandise by themselves or others' were commanded to appear at short notice before the Mayor and Aldermen, either themselves or their attorneys 'in order to be in lot and scot with other commoners of the City' under penalty of losing their franchise.[46] As we have seen,*g* the meaning of the phrase 'scot and lot' is obscure, and this order, alas, does not make it any clearer!

On quite a different subject—at the famous meeting of the Common Council on 29th January 1384—it was ordained and agreed 'that thenceforth there shall be no Mayor in the City unless he shall have previously been Sheriff, *so that he may be tried as to his*

---

f This decree followed the repeal of the Statute 37 Edward III, cap. 5 (in which the Grocers had been involved) providing that merchants should deal in one sort of merchandise only. It was ordained that if *anyone* had been admitted to the freedom of the City in some one mistery, and afterwards wished to pursue some other mistery, he should be allowed to do so. He was also permitted to trade in all kinds of merchandise at his will without any hindrance.[41]

g See note *l*, page 34.

governance and bounty before he attain to the estate of Mayoralty,[47] a wise and prudent rule which, as every Liveryman knows, is still part of the City's constitution.

In September 1388, the year in which 'the Merciless Parliament' condemned Nicholas Brembre to death for high treason, another Parliament met at Cambridge when 'for certain reasons laid before the King and his Council'[48] an enquiry was demanded into the privileges of the chartered crafts and of the unchartered associations (conveniently referred to as 'social guilds') formed solely for religious and social purposes. The existence of guilds and fraternities throughout the country was said to be responsible for a great deal of unrest, and in London it had long been the practice to issue proclamations against assemblies, congregations, conspiracies, conventicles and covines of which some examples for the years 1383 to 1385[h] are given in *Letter-book H*.[49] On 1st November (1388) a writ was sent to the Mayor and Sheriffs of London directing them to make proclamation for all Masters, Wardens and 'Overlookers' (or Surveyors) of misteries and crafts in the City and suburbs to bring their charters or letters patent from the King or his progenitors into Chancery before 2nd February. Another writ was sent on the same day to the Sheriffs of London (as well as to the Sheriffs of every shire in England) calling for returns from the social guilds.[50] In the first mayoralty of Nicholas Brembre[i] the Masters of Misteries who held Charters from the Crown had been ordered by the Mayor, Aldermen and 'the whole Common Council' to surrender them forthwith to the Mayor and the Chamberlain of the Guildhall. Only the Fishmongers failed to comply and they appear to have submitted to the order later.[51] On 23rd and 24th January (1389) the Chamberlain handed back to their owners the Charters of the

---

h   The prohibition against covines and conspiracies and (on one occasion) conventicles, was absolute. The other meetings could be held only with the leave of the Mayor or the Mayor and Aldermen.

i   21st March 1377 to 13th October 1378.

Fig. 32. The Shield of the Worshipful Company of Saddlers.

Drapers, Goldsmiths, Skinners, Tailors, Saddlers and Girdlers (six of the eight misteries which, as we have seen, possessed royal charters at this date) for production before the King and his Council,[52] so that these six misteries were certainly in a position to obey the writ, but no return of any mistery survives, if any was ever made. A limited number of returns to the second writ are extant, but neither investigation appears to have been followed by any definite action. It is indeed doubtful if the returns were even read![53]

The advantages of recognition by the Crown, in the face of interference by the civic authorities, were nevertheless apparent, and in a very short time the men of five separate crafts improved their position by obtaining Royal Charters, of which four were given direct to their misteries and one was granted to the religious fraternity with which their mistery was closely allied. On 30th July 1390 an Inspeximus Charter was obtained by the Tailors and Linen Armourers.[54] This was followed in 1392 by a Charter to the Guild or Fraternity of Corpus Christi favoured by the Skinners.[55] In 1394 Letters Patent were granted to the Goldsmiths[56] and in the same year to the Mercers—their earliest recorded Charter.[57] The Saddlers got their grant in 1395.[58] The last three Charters were, as we shall see, in the true sense, *Charters of Incorporation*, conferring,

as they did, *perpetual succession* on the recipients—an element com-
pletely missing from earlier grants.[j]

During the 'nineties the Tallow Chandlers are again included in
the lists of Masters sworn before the Mayor and Aldermen to rule
their misteries. The first attendance was on 4th November 1393[60]
and the second on 24th November 1394.[61] Different men were
sworn on each occasion, seeming to indicate that at this period our
Masters changed each year.[k]

Those named in 1393 were our old friend, Thomas Frankeleyn,
accompanied by John atte Lee (see Appendix L, note *a*), Robert
Lodwyk (or Lodewyk) and Thomas Reygate, in that order. John
was probably related to William atte Lee, one of our Masters in
1377. He was certainly a kinsman of another John atte Lee, both
men being chandlers. Master John is called John atte Lee, senior,
when obtaining his discharge from serving on juries for the usual
reason in 1412[63] and again in his will enrolled in the following
year, from which we learn a good deal about the testator's
property interests. He owned 'divers land, tenements, rents,
reversions, etc.' in the parishes of St Andrew upon Cornhill (St
Andrew Undershaft) and St Dionisius de Bakchirche (St Dionis
Backchurch, in Billingsgate Ward) and elsewhere, as well as
'certain messuages and a tenement' in the parish of St Botolph
Without Aldgate, which he left to his kinsmen, and certain rents
in the parish of All Hallows de Stanyngchirche (All Hallows
Staining, in Langbourne Ward).[64] From Robert Lodwyk's will
enrolled in 1407 it appears that he owned lands and tenements in the
parish of St John upon Wallbrook, in which our Commoner of
the 'eighties, John Brokholl, also had an interest.[65] Thomas Reygate at one time owned houses in Thames Street in the parish of
St Botolph Billingsgate.[66] He was also the owner of certain shops
in the parish of St Leonard Eastcheap,[67] the reversion of which he

---

[j]   The observation of Sir John Watney, one-time clerk of the Mercers Company (the
premier Guild of London), that 'previous to the Charter of Richard II the Mercers did
not pretend to be a Corporation of themselves, but only participants with other
Companies in the privileges and common charges of the City', is worth recording in
this connection.[59]

[k]   As did the four Masters of the Mercers at this period.[62]

left to one of his sons after the death of his wife Matilda, with remainder to another son, William.[68] We learn that Matilda later married John atte Lee (the younger)[l] to whom was committed the guardianship of William 'together with his patrimony'.[69] These chandlers, as we have already seen, were a remarkably united and friendly group of men.

Our four Masters in the following year were Michael Jut, John Busshe (or Bussh), John Fers and Laurence Derham. Michael and his wife Alice are mentioned in the *Husting Roll* for 1382 as the joint owners of a tenement in the Old Fish Market at the corner of 'Lombardeshell' (Lambeth Hill) in the parish of St Mary Magdalen,[70] which seems to be all that is known of them. It is clear from the various charitable and other bequests in the will of John Busshe that he was one of our wealthiest members.[71] He is mentioned in 1376[72] as the lessee of shops in the parish of St Nicholas at the Shambles,[m] in whose church he made provision for the maintenance of a chantry for the good of his soul and the souls of his parents. He appears to have been one of those chandlers who, like Emma Hatfeld (see Appendix G), dealt in oil, of which he left a cask, or two pipes, of 'the best' to John Simond (or Symond) chandler, provided he undertook the duties of an executor. In 1393 this John Symond was discharged from serving on juries,[73] but he lived long enough to qualify for his legacy.[n] John Fers is on record as having acquired tenements in Candlewick Ward in the lane and parish of St Martin Orgar in 1394,[75] but that is all we know of him. Laurence Derham, when obtaining a discharge from jury service in 1408, provides us with an early example of one of our men being given the full title of 'tallow chandler'.[76] Eight years earlier Richard Manhale had the same distinction,[77] but the old name took some time to disappear. We see Laurence (still with

---

l   Dr Sharpe falls into the error of confusing this John atte Lee with his kinsman of the same name (see footnote *L.-Bk. I*, p. 49).

m   The church was so named from its proximity to the butchers' quarter known as 'the Shambles'. The parish was incorporated *temp.* Henry VIII into the newly formed parish of Christ Church, Newgate Street.

n   He was still acting as an executor of another man's will in 1403.[74]

the appellation 'chaundeler') in 1394 figuring in the *Husting Rolls* apparently in a fiduciary capacity,[78] but further information regarding this Master appears to be lacking.

The next mention of Masters (or Wardens) of the Tallow Chandlers *by name* and the last until our grant of arms in 1456 occurs on 14th November 1416.[o] This time we are given only three names, those of Henry Mersch, Andrew Croweste and Thomas atte Wode,[79] a phenomenon which seems to require an explanation and to which we shall refer again later. The record is in another respect unusual. We know something of Henry Mersch (or Merssh), but little or nothing of the other two. Henry may have been related in some way to Gilbert, our Commoner of the 'eighties. A Henry atte Mersshe (see Appendix L, note *a*), without any trade designation, is mentioned in 1386 as a former tenant of properties in Bishopsgate, Ironmonger Lane and Broad Street,[80] but there is nothing to connect him with either of these men. We are on firmer ground when, in the *Plea and Memoranda Rolls* for 1435, we find the record of a bond of Thomas Hawkyn, grocer, to Henry Merssh, tallow chandler, in the sum of £11, that he would indemnify our man in case eleven weys of Bay *Salt* (from the Bay of Bourgneuf near La Rochelle) acquired from Thomas should prove not to have been 'customed', in fraud of the King and his custom.[81] Here we have another instance of a tallow chandler dealing in a commodity which was normally the province of the Salters. The puzzling case of Thomas atte Wode is discussed in Appendix L.

When we come to consider the many acts of violence committed in these tragic times we find that the catalogue of offences by men of the crafts, or of which they were suspected, is indeed a lengthy one.

Among the London rebels at the time of the Peasants' Revolt of 1381 no less than twenty-three organized misteries are mentioned, although there is good reason for believing that these men were

---

o   The lists of Masters of Misteries sworn to office are broken off with the record of 3rd November 1394 and are not resumed until October 1415. We shall have occasion later to mention 'Masters and Wardens' [un-named] of our Mistery in 1427 and 'Masters' alone [un-named] in 1442. In 1456, as the reader will learn, we find ourselves with four 'Keepers' or 'Wardens'.

mostly of humble origin.[82] No tallow chandler is named, but there are many men with no trade designation.

In January 1384, only seven months before his first trial which took place at Reading,[83] John de Northampton had bound himself in the sum of £5,000 to keep the peace.[84] He was followed during the space of nine months by another draper, a goldsmith, two skinners, a tailor, a haberdasher, four saddlers, three cordwainers, a cutler and a joiner, who likewise bound themselves in sums ranging from £40 to £300. Our John Bussh was one of the joiner's mainpernors.[85]

In September[p] Northampton was tried for the second time with two of his supporters, Richard Norbury and John More (both mercers), convicted and sentenced to ten years' imprisonment, after first being condemned to death.[87] On 2nd October the King's writ was sent to the Mayor to make proclamation in the City forbidding anyone to bear arms contrary to the King's peace.[88] The

Fig. 33. Knights jousting (Royal MS. 14 E iii).

proclamation, which followed a few days later, included the prohibition to which the reader has already been referred against attending elections without a summons.[89] Both orders are recited in an entry in the *Plea and Memoranda Roll*,[q] from which we learn that there were present in Guildhall at this time, in addition to the Mayor, Aldermen, Sheriffs and good men of the Wards duly summoned for the election of the Mayor, 'certain persons *of the*

---

p   The date according to Higden (*Polychron* IX, 48) was 10th September 1384.[86]

q   The order prohibiting the bearing of arms is recited in full as follows: 'That no one of whatsoever rank or condition should go armed or wearing headplate or jack [a defensive coat] or should lead an armed force against the King's peace.'

middle sort belonging to divers misteries'. It was said that these persons 'forgetting themselves and having no respect for, or fear of, the proclamation, and being banded together in a great congregation, made a great clamour and outcry to the great affray of the Mayor, Alderman, and Commonalty'.[90] Next we are told that divers good men of several misteries made enquiries as to the evildoers, and afterwards produced the names of certain men of their misteries who were suspected, 'while others of the guilty persons were taken and others again surrendered themselves, of whom some were mainprised and others delivered under bail'.[r] There were offenders in the ranks of the Mercers, the Goldsmiths and the Tailors, the Masters of whose misteries themselves brought the culprits before the Mayor and Aldermen for judgment. At least forty-six other culprits are found among the Armourers (seventeen), Tailors (eight), Cordwainers (five), Goldsmiths (five), Cutlers (three), Grocers, Skinners, Haberdashers, Fullers, Barbers, Broderers, Leathersellers and Pinners. Two of the offending cordwainers were reported to the Mayor and Aldermen by the Masters of their mistery. The trials covered a period of twenty-one months.[91] The lists of offenders differ from those of the earlier period in that not more than eight men are mentioned whose trade designations are lacking, and there is nothing to identify any of them with our Mistery.

The turn of Nicholas Brembre, 'that false knight of London',[92] to stand his trial with four others[s]—all favourites of the King—at the hands of the lords appellant,[t] came in February 1388. The events which followed the trial have puzzled historians. Richard, then only twenty-one years old, must have been stunned at the

---

r   The distinction between bail and mainprise is noted by Blackstone, *Commentaries*, as follows: 'Bail are only sureties that the parties be answerable for the special matter for which they stipulate; mainpernors are bound to produce him [the defendant] to answer all charges whatsoever.' See *Pl. & M. Rolls*, 1413–37, p. 45, footnote 1, where the editor discusses the correctness of this distinction, which legal writers have either denied or claimed that it was soon lost sight of.

s   Alexander Nevil *Archbishop of York*, Robert Vere *Duke of Ireland*, Michael de la Pole *Earl of Suffolk* and Robert Tresilian *Lord Chief Justice of England*.

t   The King's youngest uncle, Thomas of Woodstock *Duke of Gloucester*, Thomas Arundel *Bishop of Ely* and Thomas Beauchamp *Earl of Warwick*, joined later by Henry Bolingbroke *Earl of Derby* and Thomas Mowbray *Earl of Nottingham*.

successful prosecution of his friends on charges of giving false counsel and bringing ruin and humiliation to the realm. He must have longed for revenge; yet, with one brief interlude, an atmosphere of harmony seems to have prevailed for the next eight years. In the summer of 1392 a quarrel broke out between the King and the Londoners,[93] in consequence of which the City was taken for a short while into his hands and a Warden was appointed in place of the Mayor[94] for the first time in seventy years. But on 21st August Richard was given an ovation when paying a visit to the capital. According to a contemporary letter-writer, on returning to Westminster by water on the following day certain of the crafts accompanied the King and Queen in shouls[u] and barges. There was much music and dancing and drinks were pressed on the royal couple, who returned the compliment by inviting their hosts to drink at the palace.[95] Unfortunately, the narrator does not name the crafts.

The young King's passive attitude, interspersed with fits of temper, makes all the more surprising his studied determination to annex the Duchy of Lancaster to the Crown. His desire to avenge himself on the appellants, in which he was successful in 1397, is understandable, but the confiscation of his cousin's inheritance on the death of Henry's father, John of Gaunt, with whom Richard seems to have been on the best of terms for some years, was an act of folly for which he was to pay with his life. He was to learn too late what little reliance could be placed on the Londoners. No sooner had Bolingbroke landed in England than the news was proclaimed throughout the City, and the Mayor, with other citizens, took horse to meet the Duke, whom they escorted to London.[96] On hearing of the landing Richard hurried back from Ireland, whence he had gone ostensibly to avenge the death of the heir presumptive to the Crown.[v] His actions thereafter are difficult to understand. He was no warrior, but how he came to be trapped so soon into submission and the 'voluntary surrender' of

---

u   'Flat-bottomed boats'. *O.E.D.*

v   Roger Mortimer, 4th Earl of March, killed in the uprising of July 1398.

Fig. 34. Parliament assembled for the deposition of Richard II.

his throne has never been satisfactorily explained.[w] According to one account the force of Londoners accompanying Henry when setting out to meet his cousin, although fully armed and horsed, numbered no more than 1,200 men.[98] Sentence of deposition was passed upon Richard without any semblance of a trial, and Henry IV's accession officially began on 30th September (1399)—the date on which he is said to have 'challenged the Crown'.[99]

Dr Sharpe's Calendar of *Letter-book H*—a particularly fruitful source of information up to now—is unhelpful in its closing stages. Some of the original folios, as its editor has pointed out, have been removed, others are left blank, and the writing on others is almost, if not entirely, illegible. When we come to consult the invaluable record of the two succeeding reigns provided by *Letter-book I* we shall witness the beginning of a primitive form of street lighting, a matter which proved to be of great importance to our Company for a period of over three hundred years.

---

w   The official version of his 'resignation' at Conway is now thought to have been a Lancastrian fable and little reliance can be placed on the official account in the parliamentary roll of events in September/October 1399.[97]

Appendix A

THE WALBROOK

The stream flowed into the City from the moor lying north of London Wall, of which a large area is now occupied by Finsbury Circus, its point of entry probably being at the lower end of Blomfield Street (as it now is)[1] where two culverts were found during excavations early in the present century;[a] whence it took a winding course through the Wards of Coleman Street, Broad Street, Cheap, Walbrook, Vintry and Dowgate.

It ran on from the Wall to the north-east corner of Throgmorton Avenue where it flowed under Carpenters' Hall, then south-west to the Church of St Margaret Lothbury and on to Grocers' Hall, where it passed beneath the eastern part of the Company's kitchen; thence south under the Church of St Mildred Poultry, west from the Stocks Market where the Mansion House now stands.

After crossing Bucklersbury it passed west of the Church of St Stephen Walbrook and west of the present street of Walbrook; thence by the west end of the Church of St John the Baptist, which stood at the north-east corner of Cloak Lane, formerly known as Horse Shoe Bridge Street, at which point the bed of the stream is said to have been as much as 248 feet wide.

Thence it made its way south under Horse Shoe Bridge (long since demolished) to become the western boundary of *Tallow Chandlers Hall*, Dowgate Hill, flowing on beneath Skinners Hall to Elbow Lane (now College Street) where there appears to have been some kind of bridge;[3] proceeding thence to what we now call *Upper* Thames Street, where it made its final crossing before entering the Thames near the water-gate known as Dowgate.

---

a   It may have had another and more westerly point of entry from a separate source.[2]

Appendix B

CASES OF THE SWORD AND BUCKLER TYPE

(1) In a case in which *William le Chaundeler* was on the jury, a number of malefactors came after vespers with swords, misericords[a] and knives to the house of one Master Henry de Derby whom they attacked; one of them was arrested with his misericord in his hand, the rest were driven away by good men of the neighbourhood.

(2) In an affray in which an Alderman had his clothes torn by a defendant caught fighting with a drawn sword in Thames Street, the culprit was condemned to come on the morrow from the place of the offence to Guildhall, with bare head, and clothed only in his tunic, in charge of two serjeants, carrying in his hand an axe;[b] on arrival he was made to hold up the axe with the hand which he had laid on the Alderman in order to expiate his offence.

(3) One Roger le Rous, charged with making a great roistering with unknown minstrels, tabor-players and trumpeters, to the grave damage and tumult of the whole neighbourhood, was fortunate enough to be acquitted.

(4) A certain chaplain in Belleryteyslane[c] '*in the rent of Matthew le Caundeler*' (sic) was arrested as a night-walker whose habit it was to make disturbances in various inns to the terror of the neighbourhood. The result of the case is not reported.

(5) Another chaplain, whose plea was that he was coming from a certain house about curfew *carrying a lantern* and that the plaintiff —one of a group of malefactors—attacked him, was found guilty of assault, seemingly against the evidence.

---

a   Misericord—so called from it being used for giving the *coup de grace* to anyone or anything wounded and at the point of death.
b   To show that he had rendered himself liable to the loss of his hand—the ancient penalty for striking an Alderman.
c   Billiter Lane.

(6) Two men who were refused permission to enter a house to indulge in buckler play were charged with attacking the wife of the occupier with their swords; it so happens that one *Henry le Sauser* was a mainpernor.

(7) A number of defendants who had been captured and put in the Tun, were charged by members of the Watch, including the beadle of the Ward, with assault; some were released on bail, others, after being mainprized to attend the Court and failing to come, were convicted; the jury found on oath that they had committed the assault when midnight was striking at St Paul's and were captured after the hue and cry had been raised by horn and voice[d] and the neighbouring Wards had come to help.

(8) In another case of assault on the Watch the defendants were fined 8*d.* each for damages, and were sent to prison for breaking the peace at night time 'to the terror of the neighbours and the scandal of the City'.

(9) A man and wife were summoned to answer the Wardens of London Bridge in a plea of trespass wherein the latter complained that the defendants had been found guilty by a jury of abetting their two sons in ill-treating the neighbours. They had promised not to harbour or maintain them in future under penalty of forfeiting their house on the Bridge. Nevertheless they had received and maintained them in assaulting their neighbours, 'and in threatening to light such a fire as would be seen by all the dwellers in London'. The couple agreed (as recorded elsewhere)[e] that if in future they were to receive and maintain their sons in any way they would surrender all right and claim to their house on the Bridge.

---

d   It was the duty of all those who saw a felony committed, or were near the scene of the crime, to take part in the arrest of the transgressor, or if unable to do so without assistance, to raise hue and cry, so that the neighbours might hear and come to their aid.

e   *L.-Bk. C*, p. 76.

Appendix C

THE REGULATIONS FOR THE ELECTION OF ALDERMEN DEFINED, AND THEIR POWERS CONFIRMED

Be it remembered that on Tuesday before the Feast of St. Botolph [17 June], 21 Edward I [AD 1293], in the presence of Sir John le Bretun, Warden of London,^{a} the whole Commonalty of the City aforesaid was assembled, viz., from each Ward the wealthier and wiser men, who each by their several Wards elected for themselves Aldermen freely, of good will and of their full consent, and the Aldermen so elected they presented to the Warden aforesaid in this form, that all and singular the things which the aforesaid Aldermen of their wisdom and discretion shall do and ordain for the government of the City and the maintenance of the King's peace, in conjunction with the Warden and their superior for the time being, shall be straitly observed, and shall be held ratified and confirmed before other provisions touching the Commonalty, without any challenge or opposition in the future; and each Ward elected its Alderman, for whom it would answer as to all his acts affecting the City, the Commune (*communam*), and its estate.

---

a The City at this date being in the King's hands.

Appendix D

THE PRIVATE LIFE OF MICHAEL THE OYNTER

I

Ward of Chepe—Monday the morrow of Clausum Pasche,[a] 5 Edward I [AD 1277], information given to the Chamberlain and Sheriffs that Symon de Wynchester, taverner, lay dead of another than his rightful death in the parish of St. Martin, in Ismongere-lane[b] in the above Ward, in the house of Robert le Surigien de Frydaystrate, in which house the said Symon kept a tavern. *Inquest thereon.* The jurors (drawn from the above Ward and the Wards of Bassieshawe and of Henry de Frowyk)[c] find that the deceased met his death in December last at the hands of his servant, Roger de Westminster, who cut off his head and secreted the body in a coal cellar, and after a while left the house, depositing the key with Hamo the Cook, a neighbour; that on the last day of the year John Doget, a taverner, and Gilbert de Colecestre called at the house and took away certain casks, with the assistance of Henry Wyting, William le Waleys, Ralph le 'Yreis', Hugh Noteman, and Stephen de 'Ryminge', porters,[d] and then left the house, the said John Doget taking the key with him; that the house remained empty until Tuesday before Palm Sunday, when Master Robert aforesaid came and broke open the door, and enfeoffed *Michael le Oynter* thereof, who discovered the body.

---

a   The Sunday after Easter.

b   Ironmonger Lane.

c   Cripplegate Ward.

d   *Barem'*; perhaps for *baremannos*, biermen (Riley). The term, as applied more especially to the wine trade, appears to have given the name of 'Bermancherche' to the church of St Martin in the Vintry (Dr R. R. Sharpe).

The four nearest neighbours attached,[e] viz., Robert Schevehod[f] by Eadward le Mercer and Robert le Lung, mercer; John 'Navereathom'[g] by *William de Langele*, '*oynter*',[h] and John le Lung, 'pessoner';[i] Theywyn le Bokeler by Martin le Bukeler and *Warin le Oynter*,[j] William de Reygate, clerk, by John le Lung and Martin le Bukeler.

And John Doget was attached by Thomas Abel and Richard Curtays; Gilbert de Colecestre by Richard Scharp and Geoffrey Horn; Master Robert by Nicholas le Convers and Hugh de Gisors; *Michael le Oynter* by Nicholas de Nottone and Adam le Tayllur; Hamo the Cook by William de Donestaple, 'feliper',[k] and Eadward le Mercer; Henry Wyting, *Barem'*, by Richard de Oxford, cordwainer, and Adam le Seinturer; William le Waleys by John Monede, cordwainer, and Symon le Pipere; Ralph le 'Yreys' by Richard le Lung, *Barem'*, and Geoffrey Noteman; Hugh Noteman by Walter Skypp' and Adam le Counter (?); Stephen de 'Rominge' by John Bonholte and William de Wolcherchehawe.

2

Monday after the Invention of H. Cross [3 May] 12 Edward I [AD 1284] was read a certain writing whereby *Michael de St. Alban* and Gonilda his wife quitclaimed[l] to the Prior and Convent of

---

e   The discoverer of the corpse, as well as those who witnessed the felony (if known), and two or four neighbours were usually attached *by sureties* to appear, if required, before the Justices itinerant at their next coming to the City. On this occasion nine others concerned in the matter, including the owner of the house in which the body was found, were also attached.

f   A lane known as 'Sevedhodeslane' was situated in the Jewry, where the murderer was supposed to have taken the property he had stolen from his masters (Dr R. R. Sharpe).

g   Never-at-home.

h   Evidently another member of our oynter colony in Westchepe, although not mentioned in the Removal Order (Volume I).

i   Fishmonger.

j   See Volume I and supra page 45.

k   Skinner.

l   Quitclaim—formal renunciation or giving up of a claim.

H. Trinity, London, the land and houses in the parish of H. Trinity formerly demised to them by the said Prior and Convent for their lives. For which grant the said Prior and Convent granted to the said Michael, so long as he was content to live within the Priory without his wife, the use of a moiety of a house formerly belonging to Master Thomas Romain, together with a supply of daily food from the Convent kitchen. If the said Michael left the Convent for more than a month, he was to receive a weekly allowance of 5d. in lieu of his food, or 20s. a year if he chose to leave the Convent altogether. His wife, too, so long as she lived apart from her husband, was to receive a yearly allowance of 10s. from the Convent's cellarer, whether her husband were alive or dead; saving to the said Michael and Gonilda their right to bread and ale under a deed sealed with the conventual seal. The same annuities were to be paid to the said husband and wife if they came together again, in addition to an allowance of bread and ale. Witnesses, Sir H. de Galeys [Waleys], Mayor; Jordan Godshep and Martin Box, Sheriffs; John de Norhampton, Alderman of the Ward;[m] John de Enefeud, Thomas the Tailor, Robert de 'Coring-ho', German the clerk, John de Stanes, and others [not named].

---

m   Aldgate.

Appendix E

THE MODE AND FORM OF ELECTIONS OF MAYOR AND SHERIFFS

Edward, by the grace of God, &c., to the Mayor and Sheriffs of London greeting. Whereas by the charters of our progenitors, kings of England, it has been granted to our citizens of the City aforesaid that they may elect a Mayor and Sheriffs from among themselves whom they will, and present them, we not being at Westminster, to the Treasurer and Barons of our Exchequer, that they may be there admitted as the custom is; and such election in times past hath been accustomed to be made by the Mayor and Aldermen, and also by the more discreet [men] of the said City specially summoned and warned for the purpose. And now we have understood that certain of the common people (*populares*) and plebeians, by conspiracy had among them, perpetrating contentions (*contenciones*),[a] discords, and innumerable wicked acts in the said City by night and day, and holding clandestine meetings in private places one with another, being neither called nor summoned, have of their own accord thrust themselves into and mingled with such elections [and] by threats and clamours preventing elections being rightly made, strive to elect such as hereafter may favour their misdeeds, that their wickedness may, by reason of default of suitable government by those so elected by dissimulation, pass unpunished, to the prejudice of our crown and dignity, and also the subversion of the state of the City aforesaid and the manifest oppression of our citizens dwelling in the same. We being willing to provide for the quiet [and] tranquillity of the people our subjects, and to obviate such malice, as we are in duty

---

a   Altered by a later hand into *conuenciones* (Dr R. R. Sharpe).

bound, command you, strictly enjoining that, before the time of election of the Mayor and Sheriffs next to be elected, ye cause it to be publicly proclaimed and strictly forbidden throughout the City that any one, unless he be specially called or summoned for the purpose or be bound thereunto, shall approach there at that time, or intrude himself in the election to be made, or impede it in any way, under pain of imprisonment, from which he shall not be released without our special order. And that the said election be made by the Aldermen and other of the more discreet and power-ful citizens of the said City, as in the same it has been accustomed of old to be made. Holding as certain that if ye shall present to us, or the Treasurer and Barons of the Exchequer aforesaid, any persons elected in a different manner from that premised, we shall in no wise admit them. Witness ourself at Westminster, 4 July, the eighth year of our reign [AD 1315].

Appendix F

ORDINANCE THAT BREWERS SHALL NOT WASTE THE WATER OF THE CONDUIT IN CHEPE

At a Husting of Pleas of Land, holden on the Monday next before the Feast of St. Margaret the Virgin [20 July], in the 19th year of the reign of King Edward the Third etc., it was shown by William de Iford, the Common Serjeant, on behalf of the Commonalty, that whereas of old a certain Conduit was built in the midst of the City of London, that so the rich and middling persons therein might there have water for preparing their food, and the poor for their drink; the water aforesaid was now so wasted by brewers, and persons keeping brewhouses, and making malt, that in these modern times it will no longer suffice for the rich and middling, or for the poor; to the common loss of the whole community.

And for avoiding such common loss, it was by the Mayor and Aldermen agreed, with the assent of the Commonalty thereto, that such brewers, or persons keeping brewhouses, or making malt, shall in future no longer presume to brew or make malt with the water of the Conduit. And if any one shall hereafter presume to make ale with the water of the Conduit, or to make malt with the same, he is to lose the tankard[a] or tyne with which he shall have carried the water from the Conduit, and 40d., the first time, to the use of the Commonalty; the tankard or tyne, and half a mark, the second time; and the third time he is to lose the tankard

---

a   A large pail, or tub, for carrying water, was so called. The tankard contained about three gallons, was hooped round, and in figure like the frustum of a cone; it had a small iron handle at the upper end, and being fitted with a bung, or stopple, was easily carried on the shoulders (Riley).

or tyne, and 10s; and further, he is to be committed to prison, at the discretion of the Mayor and Aldermen there to remain.

It was also agreed at the same Husting, that the fishmongers at the Stokkes, who wash their fish therewith, shall incur the same penalty.

19 Edward III. AD 1345

Appendix G

PARTICULARS OF GOODS IN THE HOUSE OF EMMA HATFELD

with Dr A. H. Thomas' notes as printed in his
Calendar of Plea and Memoranda Rolls, 1364–81

Delivered to Matthew Langrich, fishmonger, and Margaret, daughter of William Hatfeld, chandler, on Monday after the Feast of SS. Philip and James [1 May] A° 47 Edw. III [1373]: Money in the shop, 12s; divers debts, £11 7s 9d; a barrel of Seville oil (*oille de Civile*), 30s; one barrel of *seym*,[a] 25s; a tub of Seville oil, 18s; 12 gallons of *pichsmult*,[b] 9s; 8 stones and 5 lbs of *flathegrece*,[c] 7s; 94 lbs of candles, 13s 4d; 2 pots with white grease, 3s; 7 pieces of cord, 10½d; 2 dozen and 10 halters (*chevestres*), 17d; 5 pieces of *bastilcordes*,[d] 20d; 17 panniers, 18d; ½ cwt 14 lbs of *rosyn*, 3s 4d; 20 lbs of *seu*,[e] 2s 6d; one piece of *saccloth*, 6s; 2¼ bushels of salt, 22d; pack-thread (*pacfill*) and *whippecorde*, 8d; 6 *auncers* with 4 *bolles*, 5s; one *perche*[f] of iron, 3s 4d; one lantern, 12d; 2 pieces of Sandwich cord, 10d; one tun and other vessels, 13s 4d; 4 barrels of thick *seym*, £4; one barrel *saltsmult*,[g] 35s; one

---

a   *Sc.:* seam, fat, grease.

b   Probably pitchsmolt, smelted or melted pitch, or grease and pitch.

c   Or *flachegrece*, of uncertain meaning. A *flath* was a ray or skate; *flache* in O.F. denotes weak, poor quality.

d   Of uncertain meaning.

e   Tallow.

f   A horizontal bar or peg for hanging things upon.

g   *Sc.:* saltsmolt, salt grease.

barrel of mixed (*medle*) *seym*, 33s 4d; one *tubbe* of *refus*, 23s 4d; one tub of black *seym*, 13s 4d; *pichsmult*, 5s; 231 lbs of candles, 42s; 33 lbs of green candles, 5s 6d; 6 empty tuns, 24s; 5 chests, 5s; *code*[h] and *rosyn*, 6s 8d; one *grynstone*, 12d; one iron beam with the weights, 23s 4d; 6 empty tuns, 13s 4d; 36 empty barrels, 9s; one empty tun, 8d; 11 bushels of salt of Berflet,[i] 8s 3d; 2½ qrs of coarse salt, 11s 8d; 16½ stones of *flotts*,[j] 8s 3d; 7½ stones of green seu, 7s 10½d; 12 lbs of cotton (*coton*), 10s.

Item 3 *dorsers* with cushions, *costers* and *bankers*, £6 6s 8d; 3 folding tables (*tables pliants*) and 4 plain tables with trestles, 20s; 7 *stoles*, 14d; one *target* and one *launce*, 2s; two ladders (*escheles*), 12d; *bacyns* and ewers, 30s.

Item divers pieces of cloth (*listres*) with curtains and *testers* and other things belonging to a chamber, and also a *seynte*,[k] £12 5s 2d; silver vessels, £7 15d [*sic*]; a nut (*nois*) fitted with a covercle of silver, 30s; a silver foot for a mazer cup, 8s 6d.

Item 10 *hanaps*[l] of mazer, £4 9s; table knives, 4s; napery, 20s; a candelabrum of latten, 18s.

Item divers brass pots, £4 12s; divers pails, 18s 6d; pewter vessels, 43s 6¾d; divers things of iron, 33s; divers things belonging to the *hostiel*, 40s.

Sum total £86 9s 5¼d [*sic*].

---

h   Cobbler's wax.

i   Possibly Benfleet, Co. Essex.

j   Of the same meaning as *flotagium*, skimmed fat.

k   A statuette or picture of a saint.

l   Goblets.

Appendix H

ACCOUNT OF THE KEEPERS OF THE CONDUIT
IN CHEPE
24 Edward III. AD 1350
with H. T. Riley's notes as printed in his
Memorials of London and London Life

For repairing the fountain-head, 33s. 6d.; spent another time, on examining the Conduit, when it was slandered for poison,[a] by command of the Mayor, 32s. 2d.; for bringing the pipe of the said Conduit into the Mews,[b] three men working for three days, each man receiving 8d. per day, 6s.; for ale given to them, 6d.; for mending the *spurgail*,[c] which was broken at Flete Bridge, 6s. 3½d.; for mending the pipe there, 6s. 8½d.; for mending the *spurgail*, which was broken between the Mews and the mill in the field,[d] five men working four days, each man receiving 8d. per day, 6s. 8d.;[e] paid them for drink[f] 5d. each day, 20d.; for cleansing and washing the fountain-head, twice each quarter, at 40d. each time, for the year 26s. 8d.; for mending and covering the pipe at the fountain-head, in the high road, four men working for two days, each man receiving 6d., 4s.; paid them 4d. each day for drink, 8d.; for hire of a man and his cart for two days, at 2s. per

---

a   *Esclandre de poyson.*

b   The royal Stables near Charing Cross; where the King's falcons were also 'mewed', or confined.

c   Probably a stopcock.

d   On the site, not improbably, of Great Windmill Street, Haymarket.

e   This total is incorrect.

f   These donations for drink to workmen are called, in *Letter-book G*, fol. iv (27 Edw. III), 'nonechenche' [nonschenche], probably 'noon's quench' [Dr Sharpe's note reads 'otherwise "noon-quench"']. Whence the later 'nuncheon', or luncheon.

day, 4s.; for closing and opening the Conduit, candles, and other expenses in our term, 10s. 6d.; for hire of two vadlets 24 days, to collect the money for the tankards,*g* the vadlets receiving 6d. per day, 12s.; for hire of a house for putting the tankards in, for one year, 10s.; paid for two irons for stamping the tankards, 2s. 6d; bought one *fozer*[h] of lead, which is now ready, for 8 marks and 12 pence. The said Masters account for ready money in their possession, 41s. 6d.

Also, the said Masters ask for allowance and reward for their trouble, during the time that they have been Masters of the said Conduit.

---

g See Appendix F, note *a*.

h Probably for 'fother', in London 19½ cwt.

Appendix I

ORDINANCE OF THE WAXCHANDLERS
32 Edward III. AD 1358
with H. T. Riley's notes as printed in his
Memorials of London and London Life

This Ordinance was made in the time of John de Stodeye, Mayor, at the Feast of the Nativity of St John the Baptist [24 June], in the 32nd year.—

For redress of many grievances and damages that divers folks have in many cases suffered in the City of London, as to the which remedy has not been ordained heretofore; the Mayor, Aldermen, and Sheriffs, with the assent of the good folks of the Commonalty, have ordained the Articles under-written, for the profit of the common people.—

In the first place,—it is ordained that all the Waxchandlers who are dwelling within the said city, and in the suburb, as well freeman as foreigners, who shall make torches, *cierges,*[a] *torchys,*[b] *priketz,*[c] great candles, or any other manner of wax-chandlery, for sale, shall make such torches, *cierges, torchyz, priketz,* and all other things which pertain unto their trade, of as good wax within as without, making the whole thereof of the same wax; and that they shall not put into their *wykes*[d]

---

a   Wax tapers; *torches* being twisted candles, of probably larger size.

b   A variety of the torch; perhaps the same as 'torchettes', sometimes mentioned.

c   Wax candles, for placing on a *perk*, or spike of metal.

d   Wicks.

any fat, *code*,[e] rosin, or other manner of refuse;[f] nor shall they
use old wax and worse within, and new wax without. And
that they shall not make their *wykes*, which they put into
such manner of work, of excessive weight, so as to be selling
wyke for wax, to the damage, and in deceit, of the common
people; but let their *wyke* be in accordance with the quantity
of the wax, as it reasonably ought to be. And if any wax-
chandler shall from henceforth do to the contrary of this
Ordinance, and of the same be duly convicted, the first time,
all the torches, *cierges, torchyz, priketz*, and other wax-
chandlery, that shall be found in his possession made, shall be
burnt before the door of him who shall have made the same,
at the place where he dwells, and his body shall be committed to prison; until he shall have made fine to the Commonalty, at the discretion of the Mayor and Aldermen, for
such manner of deceits and falsities committed, to the damage
of the common people and the scandal of the said city. And
on a second default, let the torches and other works be burnt
as is before ordained, and his body be put upon the pillory.
And the third time, he is to forswear the City, and all torches
and such work.

And that this Ordinance may be the more surely kept and
maintained, let there be forthwith chosen two or four of the
most lawful folks of the said trade; who shall be sworn before
the Mayor and Aldermen, lawfully to present all the defaults
that they find in their trade, from one day to another. But in
case any reputable man shall come to the aforesaid wax-
chandlers, and shall wish them to make torches, *torchiz,
prykes, cirgez* for mortuaries,[g] or other large candles, of old
and new wax, mixed together for his own use, the wax-
chandlers may have the same made at the will of the owner,
without hindrance thereof, so that he make no sale thereof,
on the pain aforesaid.

---

e   Cobbler's wax.

f   *Litour.*

g   Funeral obsequies, or rites in remembrance of the dead. Hence probably the term
     'mortar', still applied to a certain kind of candle.

H

Appendix J

MONIES RECEIVED FROM DIVERS MISTERIES AS
A PRESENT TO THE KING

	£	s	d
Mercers	40	0	0
Drapers	40	0	0
Fishmongers	40	0	0
Skinners	40	0	0
Vintners	33	6	8
Grocers	31	6	8
Butchers	23	0	0
Goldsmiths	20	0	0
Tailors	20	0	0
Brewers	14	6	8
Chandlers	8	0	0
Ironmongers	7	18	4
Girdlers	6	13	4
Brasiers	6	13	4
Cordwainers	6	13	4
Poulterers	6	13	4
Saddlers	5	0	0
Pewterers	5	0	0
Cutlers	4	0	0
Tanners	3	11	0
Curriers	3	6	8
Pouchmakers	3	6	8
Armourers	3	0	0
Bowyers	3	0	0
Wax Chandlers	2	0	0
Spurriers	2	0	0
Glovers	1	0	0
Individual subscribers	48	13	4

£428   9s   4d

Appendix K

TABLE

Showing the attendances of men of the Mistery of Tallow Chandlers at meetings
of the Common Council from 31st July 1384 to 31st August 1388

31st July 1384	*August 1384*	*13th October 1384* *(Election of Nicholas Brembre)*
Richard Brangwayn (Master 1377) Thomas Mordone Richard Manhale John Sandhurst William atte Lee (Master 1377) Gilbert Mersshe Richard Willesdone John Goldryng Thomas Chaundeler	Richard Brangwayn (Master 1377) Thomas Mordone Richard Manhale John Sandhurst William atte Lee (Master 1377) Gilbert Mersshe Richard Willesdone John Goldryng Thomas Chaundeler	Richard Brangwayn (Master 1377) Richard Manhale John Sandhurst William atte Lee (Master 1377) Gilbert Mersshe Richard Willesdone John Goldryng Thomas Chaundeler John Cook (or Cok)
1384/5 *(eighth year of Richard II)*	*18th July 1385*	*1385/6* *(ninth year of Richard II)*
Richard Brangwayn (Master 1377) Richard Manhale William atte Lee (Master 1377) Gilbert Mersshe Richard Willesdone John Goldryng Thomas Chaundeler John Cook Thomas Frankeleyn (Master 1377 and 1393)	Richard Manhale John Sandhurst Richard Willesdone Thomas Frankeleyn (Master 1377 and 1393)	Richard Manhale John Sandhurst
March 1386 [a]	*1387* *(tenth year of Richard II)*	*31st August 1388*
Richard Manhale William atte Lee (Master 1377) Richard Willesdone John Goldryng John Cook	Richard Manhale Thomas Frankeleyn (Master 1377 and 1393)	Richard Manhale John Sandhurst William atte Lee (Master 1377) Roger Haukewelle

[a]   It was decided at this meeting that it would be better for the peace of the City that
John de Northampton, John More and Richard Norbury should be kept at a distance
of 100 miles from London.

Appendix L

THE CASE OF THOMAS ATTE WODE

The name by which this Master was known belongs to a group of *local surnames* formed from topographical elements denoting the person's place of residence, preceded by the word 'atte' (at the).[a]

An unusual, if not unique, feature of the present case is that we should find two men of different misteries, each bearing the name Thomas atte Wode, officiating as Master of his mistery in the same year, one a hurer, capper or kapmaker, the other a tallow chandler.

We meet Thomas atte Wode, the hurer, on three occasions in 1394, as one of four Masters *and Surveyors* of the Mistery of Hurers concerned in punishing the makers and sellers of false caps,[1] and in April of that year the same four men are sworn to duty as 'Masters'.[2] In October 1416 Thomas appears again—as first named of four Masters of *Kapmakers*[3]—and *our* Master, Thomas atte Wode, is sworn, with two others, as we have seen, in the following month.[4]

---

[a] The following six examples occur in the text, including the one with which we are particularly concerned in this Appendix.

John *atte Holmes* de Enfeld	Page 40
Holme, Holmes	A holm, an islet in, or flat land beside, a river
William *atte Lee* ⎫	
John *atte Lee* ⎭	Pages 74, 90
Ley, Legh, Lea	A meadow, a grassy plain
Gilbert *atte Mersshe* ⎫	
Henry *atte Mersshe* ⎭	Pages 79, 92
Mersh, Merssh	A marsh, i.e. swamp, bog
William *atte Noke* (atten oak)	Page 47
Oak, Oak tree	M.E. oke (as with 'atten' ash)
Henry *atte Rothe*, Roche	Page 41
O.E. 'rop'	Clearing (dweller in a). Distinguishable from O.F. 'roche' (at the rock)
Thomas *atte Wode*	Page 92
Wode	A wood

In London, a man's trade description frequently followed his surname, by which designation we recognize the capper Thomas more than once,[b] but there are other occasions when we cannot tell which man (if either) is meant. We know from their testamentary dispositions that there were in fact two different persons of the same name. Otherwise we might be tempted to assume that we are dealing with one man carrying on at the same time two entirely different trades, in both of which he attained the same distinction. We are saved from this unlikely conclusion by the knowledge that Thomas, the hurer, is so described in his will enrolled in 1430,[6] and that Thomas atte Wode, tallow chandler, is so called in the register of wills kept in the Commissiary Court of London.[7]

It was not uncommon for a man to have an alias, or second surname, but in this instance none has come to light. Thomas atte Wode, alias 'Boterwyk',[c] is mentioned in 1386,[8] but he cannot be our man, nor can he be the capper, for Boterwyk had a wife Alice and a son John, both of whom are named in the will of Thomas atte Wode enrolled in 1397.[9] In the result we are left with only one positive piece of information about our Master. The Court record for the year 1426 (supra) tells us that he owned property in the old parish of St Andrew Holborn.

---

b   He was appointed guardian to two infant children and named as their father's executor in 1419.[5]

c   Or Butterwick (butter farm or dairy), indicating that he came from one of the places of this name, perhaps East or West Butterwick, Co. Lincoln.

Authorities

(For Abbreviations see page 7)

LONDON AT THE TURN OF THE THIRTEENTH CENTURY

Page	Note	
9 (footnote *a*)	1	*L.-Bk. A*, pp. 223–4.
11	2	On folios clv b–clix b of *Letter-book D* is entered a series of articles which appear in *Liber Custumarum* (fos. 201–6b) under the heading 'Ceux sount les articles des auncienes usages de assise de pain et de cervoise et dautre vitaille et de plusurs mestiers de la Cite de Loundres qe deivent chescun an apres le Sein Michele estre cries par mi la dite cite' (*L.-Bk. D*, p. 298). These articles of ancient usage, with some exceptions, are again recorded (with the language considerably altered) in *Liber Albus*, fos. 198a–202a (*Lib. Alb.*, pp. 260–80; Riley, *Liber Albus*, pp. 228–43).
11	3	Riley, *Liber Albus*, p. 243.
11	4	*L.-Bk. D*, p. 251; Riley, *Memorials*, p. 83 and footnote.
12 (footnote *f*)	5	*L.-Bk. B*, p. 242; Ibid., pp. 34–5.
12	6	Riley, *Liber Albus*, p. 232.
12 (footnote *h*)	7	See *Letter-book A*, fo. 127.
12	8	*Pl. & M. Rolls*, 1323–64, Introduction, p. xvi.
12	9	*L.-Bk. A*, p. 213.

Page	Note	
13	10	P.R., 1281–92, p. 94.
13	11	Ibid., p. 80.
13	12	L.-Bk. C, p. 84.
14	13	L.-Bk. B, pp. 1–12.
14	14	Riley, *Liber Albus*, p. 240.
14	15	Ibid., pp. 241–2.
15	16	„ pp. 14–15.
15	17	*Lib. Cust.*, Part I, p. 338.
15 (footnote *o*)	18	*Mediaeval London, From Commune to Capital*, by Professor Gwyn Williams (1963), p. 254.
15	19	This is the record in the *Liber Albus*.
15	20	*Chron. Edw. I and Edw. II* (Ann. Lond.), p. 94.
15	21	These are the words used in the preamble as printed in the *Statutes of the Realm*.
16	22	See in general the 'Statutes for the City of London' following the Statute of Winchester, as printed on pages 102–4 in the *Statutes of the Realm*. They roughly correspond to the articles (undated) included with a number of other enrolments for the year 1293–4 on pages 15–17 of *L.-Bk. C*. From the references to a Warden (instead of a Mayor) the original articles were evidently issued when the City was in the King's hands, and probably date from the year 1285, the later version being a confirmation. Some of the articles (referred to as 'ordinances') are given in a different form in Riley, *Liber Albus*, pages 245–6. Some others were in the main a repetition of Waleys' articles as they appear in pages 228–43 of Riley.
16	23	Riley, *Liber Albus*, p. 244.
16	24	Ibid., pp. 250–1.
17	25	See 'City Cleaning in Mediaeval London' by Ernest L. Sabine, printed in *Speculum*, Vol. viii, pp. 19–43.

Page	Note	
17	26	C.R., 1349–54, pp. 65–6.
17	27	Riley, *Liber Albus*, p. 237.
17	28	Ibid., p. 251.
18	29	See 'Butchering in Mediaeval London', printed in *Speculum*, Vol. xii, pp. 335–53.
19	30	The three orders mentioned in this paragraph are all contained in the 'Statutes for the City of London', op. cit.
19	31	C.R., 1288–96, p. 45.
19	32	L.-Bk. C, p. 8.
19	33	'Statutes for the City of London', op. cit. See *Pl. & M. Rolls*, 1323–64, Introduction, p. xxi.
19	34	See *L.-Bk. A*, p. 198. Thomas Romeyn and William de Leyre, elected Sheriffs of London and Middlesex 'by the Commonalty of the City'.
20	35	L.-Bk. B, pp. 240–1; L.-Bk. C, pp. 20–1.
20	36	L.-Bk. C, p. 22.
20	37	Ibid., pp. 23–4.
21	38	L.-Bk. B, p. 242; Riley, *Memorials*, pp. 35–6.
21	39	Ibid., p. 240.
21	40	„ pp. 242–3.
22	41	See 'The Confirmation of the Charters, 1297' by H. Rothwell, *English Historical Review*, lx (1945).
22	42	For the Londoners' special grounds for complaint see Selden Society Vol. 35 (1918), *Select cases before the King's Council*, 1243–1482, pp. liii–lvi.
22	43	L.-Bk. B, pp. 243–4.
22	44	Ibid., p. 212.
22	45	„ p. 213.
22 (footnote *u*)	46	Beaven, Part I, p. 250.
22	47	L.-Bk. B, p. 213.

Page	Note	
23	48	L.-Bk. B, p. 217; Riley, *Memorials*, pp. 36–7; C.R., 1296–1302, p. 164. The writ was a reissue of the writ of 1281 with the addition of the final sentence. See Dr A. H. Thomas' Introduction to his *Calendar of Plea and Memoranda Rolls*, 1323–64, p. xvi.
23 (footnote *w*)	49	See L.-Bk. C, p. 38 (footnote).
23	50	Ibid., p. 107.
23	51	,, pp. 50–1, 77–8, 80.
23	52	'Procedure of Inquisition and Delivery', L.-Bk. D, pp. 262–7; Riley, *Memorials*, pp. 86–9.
24	53	L.-Bk. D, p. 266.
24 (footnote *bb*)	54	L.-Bk. C, pp. 69–71.
24	55	Ibid., p. 18.
24	56	L.-Bk. E, p. 156–8.
24 (footnote *cc*)	57	L.-Bk. D, p. 229.
24	58	Pl. & M. Rolls, 1364–81, pp. 209–10.
24	59	L.-Bk. F, p. 260.
25	60	E.M.C.R., p. 214.

THE GROWING POWER OF THE CRAFTS

Page	Note	
26	1	L.-Bk. E, pp. 12–14.
28	2	L.-Bk. D, pp. 275–6.
29	3	Ibid., p. 286.
29	4	,, p. 275.
29	5	L.-Bk. D, pp. 283–4.
29	6	,, p. 284.
29	7	,, p. 283.
29	8	L.-Bk. E, p. 16.
30	9	L.-Bk. A, pp. 209–10, and see Dr Sharpe's Introduction, p. xi.

Page	Note	
30	10	*L.-Bk. C*, pp. 1–2.
30	11	Ibid., p. 2.
30	12	*L.-Bk. B*, pp. 237–9.
30	13	*C.W.C.H.*, Part I, p. 184, Roll 35 (29).
(footnote *c*)		
30	14	*L.-Bk. A*, p. 158; *L.-Bk. B*, pp. 265–6.
31	15	*L.-Bk. B*, p. 238.
31	16	*L.-Bk. A*, pp. 169–70.
31	17	Ibid., p. 146.
31	18	*L.-Bk. C*, pp. 44–50; and see Dr Sharpe's Introduction, p. xii.
31	19	Ibid., p. 239.
31	20	*L.-Bk. E*, p. 197.
31	21	Ibid., pp. 126–9.
31	22	,, pp. 93–4.
31	23	See *L.-Bk. E*, pp. 141–2.
31	24	*L.-Bk. E*, pp. 80–1.
(footnote *d*)		
,,	25	*L.-Bk. C*, p. 173.
32	26	*L.-Bk. D*, pp. 14–15.
32	27	*C.W.C.H.*, Part I, p. 269, Roll 45 (144).
(footnote *f*)		
,,	28	*L.-Bk. B*, p. 199.
32	29	See *The Household of Edward IV*, edited by A. R. Myers, 1959, Glossary, p. 276.
(footnote *g*)		
32	30	*L.-Bk. D*, p. 22.
32	31	*L.-Bk. D*, pp. 24–6.
32	32	,, p. 23.
32	33	,, p. 26.
33	34	*The French Chronicle of London*, Riley's translation, p. 252.
33	35	*L.-Bk. E*, p. 105. See the editor's footnote.
34	36	Ibid., p. 134.
34	37	For an English translation of the Letters Patent see *Historical Charters*, pp. 45–50, by Walter de Gray Birch. Note, however, the

Page	Note	

error in translation made by Strype in his edition of Stow's Survey and repeated by the author, to which Dr Sharpe draws attention on page vi of the Introduction of his Calendar of *Letter-book D*. The ordinance, in so far as the same related to the admission of 'foreigners' to the freedom, was reaffirmed in December 1326 (*L.-Bk. E*, p. 214).

Page	Note	
34 (footnote *l*)	38	Riley, *Liber Albus*, p. 235 (footnote).
„	39	See *L.-Bk. E*, p. 285 (footnote).
34 (footnote *m*)	40	*L.-Bk. G*, p. 20 (footnote).
35	41	Ibid., p. 20.
35	42	*The French Chronicle of London*, op. cit., p. 253.
35	43	*L.-Bk. D*, p. 30.
35	44	Ibid., pp. 30–1.
35 (footnote *o*)	45	For an account of the proceedings, see Dr Sharpe's *London and the Kingdom* (1894), Vol. I, pp. 143–8.
35	46	*Lib. Cust.*, Part I, p. 378; See *L.-Bk. D*, p. 31 (footnote) and *L.-Bk. E*, p. 138 (footnote).
35	47	*L.-Bk. E*, p. 144.
35	48	Ibid., p. 214.
36	49	*Pl. & M. Rolls*, 1323–64, pp. 14–17.
36	50	*The French Chronicle of London*, op. cit., p. 263.
37	51	*Chron. Edw. I and Edw. II* (Ann. Lond.), p. 318.
37	52	*Pl. & M. Rolls*, 1323–64, pp. 11–12.
37	53	Ibid., p. 12.
37 (footnote *r*)	54	„ p. xxxiii.
37	55	See *Historical Charters*, pp. 52–8.
38	56	Tailors and Linen Armourers: *P.R.*, 1327–30, p. 29; *L.-Bk. F*, p. 52.

Page	Note	
		Girdlers: *P.R.*, 1327–30, p. 40; *Pl. & M. Rolls*, 1323–64, p. 39.
		Goldsmiths: *P.R.*, 1327–30, pp. 42–3; *Pl. & M. Rolls*, 1323–64, p. 61.
		Skinners: *P.R.*, 1327–30, p. 34; *L.-Bk. E*, p. 226.
		The Charter of the Girdlers is printed in Riley, *Memorials*, at pp. 154–6 and that of the Skinners at pp. 153–4.
38	57	*Pl. & M. Rolls*, 1323–64, p. 34.
38	58	*L.-Bk. E*, pp. 232–4.
38	59	*L.-Bk. A*, p. 86.
(footnote *u*)		
,,	60	*L.-Bk. C*, pp. 52–3.
,,	61	Ibid., p. 52.
,,	62	*L.-Bk. E*, p. 162.
39	63	I venture to suggest that the conclusion drawn from this Table by George Unwin, the learned author of the *Gilds and Companies of London* (Fourth Edition, 1963), pp. 87–8, that, with few exceptions, the craft movement did not begin to develop until the accession of Edward III, is incorrect. He points out that the list consists almost entirely of the mercantile crafts, and of the wealthy manufacturing crafts which had obtained royal charters or were shortly to do so, and that only about half a dozen lesser crafts are included. As I have endeavoured to show, the omission of many names from the Table is almost certainly an accident.
39	64	*L.-Bk. F*, pp. 5–8.
39	65	See *Historical Charters*, pp. 61–2.
(footnote *v*)		
39	66	*L.-Bk. F*, pp. 8–9.

Page	Note	
39	67	*L.-Bk. F*, p. 20. The names of those chosen from the Wards are given on pp. 21–3.
39	68	*Pl. & M. Rolls*, 1323–64, p. 189.
40	69	Ibid., pp. 100–1.
40	70	„ p. 102.
40 (footnote *w*)	71	*C.W.C.H.*, Part I, pp. 417–18, Roll 64 (14).
40	72	*L.-Bk. F*, p. 29.
40	73	Ibid., p. 128.
41	74	*Husting Rolls* (45–77), 74 dors., 29 (1347).
41	75	*C.W.C.H.*, Part II, pp. 122–3, Roll 96 (242).
41	76	*Pl. & M. Rolls*, 1364–81, pp. 158–9.
41	77	Ibid., p. 159.
41 (footnote *x*)	78	See *L.-Bk. F*, p. 180; *Pl. & M. Rolls*, 1381–1412, p. 9.
42	79	(a) John de Westwyk: *Husting Rolls* (45–77), 63 dors., 287 ff. (1336); *C.W.C.H.*, Part I, p. 522, Roll 76 (72).
		(b) Robert de Manhale: *Husting Rolls* (77–101), 84.4.31 (1355); *C.W.C.H.*, Part II, pp. 46–7, Roll 89 (179).
		(c) Henry atte Rothe: *Husting Rolls* (45–77), 63 dors., 175–6 (1336); *C.W.C.H.*, Part I, p. 513, Roll 76 (16).
42	80	*L.-Bk. F*, p. 120. He had as an associate John de Enfeld, but it is not certain that this man was our John.
42 (footnote *y*)	81	London Lay Subsidy of 1332, printed in *Finance and Trade under Edward III*, ed. G. Unwin, p. 63.
„	82	*C.R.*, 1337–9, p. 275.
42 (footnote *z*)	83	*L.-Bk. A*, p. 10. See *Variation in Surnames in Medieval London* by Eilert Ekwall, pp. 230–1, where the author refers to these two men (mistakenly, I think) as cordwainers.
42	84	*L.-Bk. B*, pp. 70–1.

Page	Note	
42	85	*L.-Bk. B*, p. 111; *E.M.C.R.*, p. 119.
42	86	*L.-Bk. B*, p. 94.
42	87	Ibid., p. 95.
42	88	*C.W.C.H.*, Part I, p. 125, Roll 25 (29).
(footnote *bb*)		
42	89	*L.-Bk. B*, p. 21.
42	90	*Pl. & M. Rolls*, 1323–64, p. 118.
43	91	Ibid. (Roll A.3, membr. 10).
(footnote *dd*)		
43	92	This appears to follow from the second of the two entries on the same page.
43	93	*C.W.C.H.*, Part I, p. 585, Roll 77 (29).
43	94	*Husting Rolls* (45–77) 72.8.71 (1345) and *C.W.C.H.*, Part I, p. 560, Roll 76 (236).
43	95	*Pl. & M. Rolls*, 1323–64, pp. 117–18.
43	96	*L.-Bk. F*, pp. 45–9.
43	97	Ibid., pp. 143–7.
44	98	*L.-Bk. G*, pp. 58–62.
44	99	*C.W.C.H.*, Part I, pp. 445–6, Roll 68 (52); *L.-Bk. F*, pp. 114–15; *Pl. & M. Rolls*, 1323–64, p. 202.
44	100	See *Husting Rolls* (Wills) 73 (25).
44	101	*L.-Bk. F*, p. 175.
44	102	*C.W.C.H.*, Part II, pp. 46–7, Roll 89 (179).
44	103	*C.W.C.H.*, Part I, p. 653, Roll 79 (70).
45	104	*L.-Bk. F*, pp. 179–80.
45	105	Ibid., pp. 303–4.
45	106	See Riley, *Memorials*, pp. 264–5.
45	107	See London Lay Subsidy of 1332, op. cit., p. 73.
45	108	*Calendar of Coroners' Rolls of the City of London*, 1300–78, pp. 269–70.
(footnote *gg*)		
46	109	*Pl. & M. Rolls*, 1364–81, p. 206.
46	110	Ibid., pp. 209–10.
46	111	„ p. 234.

Page	Note	
46	112	*Pl. & M. Rolls*, 1364-81, p. 258.
47	113	*Pl. & M. Rolls*, 1323-64, p. 162.
47	114	London Lay Subsidy of 1332, op. cit., p. 65.
47	115	*L.-Bk. F*, p. 87.
47	116	*Pl. & M. Rolls*, 1323-64, p. 22.
(footnote *hh*)		
47	117	*L.-Bk. F*, pp. 91-2.
47	118	*Pl. & M. Rolls*, 1323-64, p. 241.
48	119	*L.-Bk. G*, p. 77.
48	120	*Pl. & M. Rolls*, 1364-81, p. 124.

THE DAWN OF A NEW ERA

Page	Note	
49	1	*L.-Bk. F*, p. 162.
49 (footnote *a*)	2	See *The Medieval English Borough* by Professor James Tait (1936), p. 312. Note, however, that the author, in making the point, refers in error to an Ordinance of 28th October 1346 respecting Ward quotas for the election of Mayor and Sheriffs, etc. (*L.-Bk. F*, p. 304).
49	3	Riley, *Memorials*, pp. liii–lv.
50	4	*L.-Bk. F*, pp. 237-9.
50 (footnote *b*)	5	*The Medieval English Borough*, op. cit., p. 309.
50	6	*Pl. & M. Rolls*, 1323-64, p. 234. See the entry dated 10th April 1350.
50	7	*L.-Bk. G*, p. 3.
50	8	Ibid., pp. 22-3.
50	9	*Old London Bridge*, by Gordon Home, Appendix A, p. 334.
51	10	See the *History of the Tower Bridge and of other Bridges over the Thames built by the Corporation of London*, 1894, by Charles Welch (Librarian to the Corporation), prepared under the direction of the Bridge House Estates Committee.

Page	Note	
51	11	*History of the Tower Bridge*, oy. cit., pp. 44–5.
52	12	Ibid., p. 72.
52	13	*Mediaeval Chantries and Chantry Chapels* by G. H. Cook, p. 55.
52	14	Ibid.; *Old London Bridge*, op. cit., p. 101.
52	15	*History of the Tower Bridge and of other Bridges*, op. cit., p. 72.
52	16	*C.W.C.H.*, Part II, p. 79, Roll 91 (125); *L.-Bk. H*, p. 411.
52	17	*L.-Bk. G*, p. 92.
52	18	Ibid., p. 128; Riley, *Memorials*, pp. 301–2.
52	19	*L.-Bk. G*, p. 144.
53	20	*Journals*, 8, fo. lxxxii b.
53 (footnote *d*)	21	*Men and Measures* by Edward Nicholson (1912), p. 100.
53	22	*Repertories* 5, fo. 120* b.
54	23	25 Edward III, Stat. 5, cap. ix, confirmed in 1360 by 34 Edward III, cap. v (*Statutes of the Realm*, 20, pp. 321 and 365).
54 (footnote *f*)	24	*The Strife of the Scales* (1905), by J. A. Kingdon, pp. 8 and 16–17.
55	25	See *The Strife of the Scales*, op. cit., *passim*.
55	26	Ibid., p. 25.
55	27	*L.-Bk. D*, p. 212.
55	28	Ibid., p. 296.
55	29	*L.-Bk. G*, p. 204; *The Strife of the Scales*, op. cit., p. 5.
55	30	*L.-Bk. H*, p. 175.
55	31	*Pl. & M. Rolls*, 1364–81, p. 153.
55	32	Ibid., p. 166.
56	33	*L.-Bk. G*, pp. 171–2.
56	34	*P.R.*, 1361–4, pp. 433–4.
56	35	37 Edward III, cap. v (*Statutes of the Realm*, 20, p. 379).
57	36	*P.R.*, 1364–7, pp. 6–7.
57	37	Ibid., pp. 5–6.

Page	Note	
57	38	*P.R.*,1364–7, pp. 4–5.
57	39	*Chronica Johannis de Reading*, etc., 1346–7, ed. James Tait (1914), Introduction, p. 39.
57	40	38 Edward III, cap. ii (*Statutes of the Realm*, 20, p. 383).
58	41	*L.-Bk. G*, p. 174.
58	42	*Pl. & M. Rolls*, 1364–81, p. 5.
58	43	*L.-Bk. H*, p. 31.
58	44	*L.-Bk. G*, p. 246.
59	45	Ibid., p. 251.
59	46	„ p. 253.
59	47	*Pl. & M. Rolls*, 1364–81, p. 1.
59	48	*L.-Bk. G*, p. 264; *References respecting the Mode of Watching the City of London* (Fo. Pam. 376), prepared in connection with the City of London Police Act, 2 & 3 Vic., cap. xciiv (1839).
60	49	Riley, *Memorials*, pp. 344–5.
60	50	*L.-Bk. H*, pp. 20–1.
60	51	Ibid., p. 35.
60	52	See *Chronica Johannis de Reading*, op. cit., p. 39.
60	53	*L.-Bk. G*, p. 205.
61	54	Ibid., p. 280.
61	55	*L.-Bk. H*, p. 38.
62	56	Ibid., pp. 38–41.
62	57	See *The Medieval English Borough*, op. cit., pp. 310–11.
63	58	*L.-Bk. H.*, p. 36.
63	59	Ibid., pp. 36–7.

THE CITY UNDER MISTERY RULE

Page	Note	
64	1	*L.-Bk. H*, pp. 41–4.
65	2	*Husting Rolls* (77–101) 101.4.28 (1372); Will of John de Westwyk (*C.W.C.H.*, Part I, p. 522, Roll 76 (72)).

Page	Note	
65	3	*C.W.C.H.*, Part II, p. 337, Roll 127 (46).
65	4	*Ibid.*, p. 332, Roll 126 (84).
65	5	*Husting Rolls* (101–25), 102. dors. 17 (1373).
66	6	*L.-Bk. H*, p. 59.
66	7	*Pl. & M. Rolls*, 1364–81, p. 243.
66	8	*L.-Bk. H*, p. 41.
66	9	Riley, *Liber Albus*, pp. 290–2.
66 (footnote *c*)	10	*Boutell's Heraldry*, revised by C. W. Scott-Giles and J. P. Brooke-Little (1966), pp. 246–7.
67	11	*L.-Bk. H*, pp. 64–5.
67	12	*Historical Charters*, pp. 65–6. The date is, however, incorrectly given as 12th November 1376.
67	13	*L.-Bk. H*, pp. 59–60.
68	14	*Ibid.*, p. 58.
68	15	,, pp. 88–9.
68	16	,, p. 231.
68	17	,, p. 408; 17 Richard II, cap. xi (*Statutes of the Realm*, 21, p. 91).
69	18	Riley, *Liber Albus*, pp. 422–4.
69	19	See Dr Sharpe's *London and the Kingdom*, Vol. I, pp. 210–11.
69	20	*L.-Bk. H*, pp. 60–1.
69	21	*Ibid.*, p. 78.
69	22	4th December 1376 (*Historical Charters*, pp. 67–9).
69	23	*L.-Bk. H*, p. 86.
69	24	*Ibid.*, p. 90.
69	25	*Statute of Gloucester*, 2 Richard II, cap. i (*Statutes of the Realm*, 21, p. 7).
70	26	*Rot. Parl.*, Vol. 3, pp. 225–7.
70	27	*L.-Bk. H*, p. 137.
70	28	*Ibid.*, p. 155.
70	29	,, p. 156.
70	30	,, p. 169.

Page	Note	
71	31	6 Richard II, cap. x (*Statutes of the Realm*, 21, p. 28).
71	32	*L.-Bk. H*, pp. 219–20.
71	33	Ibid., pp. 251, 276.
71	34	7 Richard II, cap. xi (*Statutes of the Realm*, 21, p. 34).
71	35	*L.-Bk. H*, p. 229.
72	36	Ibid., pp. 227–8.
72	37	„ p. 277.
72	38	„ pp. 237–40.
72	39	„ p. 277. The date is dependent on which of two Feast Days (that of St Luke or St Lucie) is named in this entry as the day of the meeting. See Dr Sharpe's footnote.
73	40	*L.-Bk. H*, p. 347.
73	41	*L.-Bk. I*, pp. 71–2.
73	42	*L.-Bk. H*, p. 251.
73	43	*L.-Bk. K*, p. 288.
73	44	*L.-Bk. L*, p. 73.
73	45	Ibid., p. 132.
74 (footnote *n*)	46	Statute 11 Geo. I, cap. 18.
74	47	*Pl. & M. Rolls*, 1381–1412, pp. 29–31.
74	48	*L.-Bk. H*, pp. 76–7.
75	49	Ibid., p. 238.
75	50	„ p. 237.
75	51	*Husting Rolls* (101–5) 117. dors. 26 (1388); *C.W.C.H.*, Part II, p. 355, Roll 132 (6).
75	52	*L.-Bk. H*, pp. 123–6.
75	53	*Husting Rolls* (101–5) 109.8.50 (1380).
76	54	*L.-Bk. G*, p. 306.
76	55	*Husting Rolls* (101–25) 113. dors. 50 (1384).
76	56	*L.-Bk. H*, p. 402.
76	57	Ibid., p. 328.
76	58	*Husting Rolls* (77–101) 94. dors. 27 (1365).
77	59	*C.W.C.H.*, Part II, p. 79, Roll 91 (125).

Page	Note	
77	60	*C.W.C.H.*, Part II, p. 369, Roll 134 (77).
77	61	*L.-Bk. H*, p. 108.
77	62	Ibid., pp. 123–6.
77	63	*C.W.C.H.*, Part II, p. 258, Roll 114 (150). See also *Husting Rolls* (101–25) 112. dors. 113 (1384).
77	64	Riley, *Memorials*, p. 371.
77	65	*Pl. & M. Rolls*, 1381–1412, p. 70.
78	66	Ibid., p. 82.

THE AFTERMATH

Page	Note	
79	1	*C.W.C.H.*, Part II, pp. 306–7, Roll 122 (41). See also *Husting Rolls* (101–25) 120. dors. 50 (1391).
79	2	*Husting Rolls* (101–25) 107.25.172 (1379); 113.18.99 (1385); 114.1.6 (1385); 116. dors. 22 (1387). See also Index to *Testamentary Records in the Commissary Court of London*, ed. Marc Fitch, Vol. I, p. 123.
79	3	*L.-Bk. H*, pp. 421–2.
79	4	*Pl. & M. Rolls*, 1381–1412, pp. 84–8.
79	5	*Husting Rolls* (77–101) 93.22.118 (1365).
79	6	*C.W.C.H.*, Part II, pp. 266–7, Roll 116 (91).
80	7	*Husting Roll* (Wills), 103 (128) and *C.W.C.H.*, Part II, p. 175, Roll 103 (128).
80	8	*Pl. & M. Rolls*, 1381–1412, pp. 91–2.
81	9	*L.-Bk. H*, pp. 269–71.
81	10	*Husting Rolls* (126–75) 127. dors. 44 (1398).
81	11	*L.-Bk. H*, p. 278.
81	12	See the deed cited at 10 supra.
81	13	*L.-Bk. H*, p. 428.
81	14	Ibid., p. 92.
81	15	„ p. 128.
81 (footnote *b*)	16	Riley, *Memorials*, pp. 419–20 (from *Letter-book H*, fo. lxxix b).

Page	Note	
Page	*Note*	
81	17	*L.-Bk. H*, p. 266.
82	18	Riley, *Memorials*, p. 488 (from *Letter-book H*, fo. cc).
82	19	*L.-Bk. H*, p. 232.
83	20	Riley, *Memorials*, p. 433 (from *Letter-book H*, fo. cxi).
83	21	*L.-Bk. H*, p. 153.
83	22	Riley, *Memorials*, p. 424 (from *Letter-book H*, fo. xcv).
83	23	Riley, *Memorials*, p. 466 (from *Letter-book H*, fo. cxlvi).
83	24	Higden, *Polychron*, ix, p. 217. (See *Letter-book H*, p. 348, footnote.)
84	25	*L.-Bk. H*, pp. 347–8.
84	26	1380. *L.-Bk. H*, p. 157.
		1387. Ibid., p. 293.
		„ „ p. 322.
		1393. Riley, *Memorials*, pp. 534–5 (from *L.-Bk. H*, fo. cclxxxvii).
84	27	1381. *L.-Bk. H*, p. 173.
		1385. Ibid., p. 274.
		1386. „ p. 289.
		„ „ p. 296.
84	28	*L.-Bk. H*, p. 338.
84	29	*The Fourteenth Century*, 1307–1399, by May McKisack, p. 466.
84	30	*L.-Bk. H*, p. 373.
84	31	Ibid., p. 405.
84	32	„ p. 162.
84	33	„ p. 235.
85	34	„ pp. 257–9.
85	35	„ pp. 259–60.
86	36	„ p. 423.
86	37	„ pp. 442–3.
86	38	*L.-Bk. I*, p. 63.
86	39	*L.-Bk. K*, pp. 189–90.

Page	Note	
86	40	*L.-Bk. K*, pp. 165–6.
87	41	*L.-Bk. G*, pp. 203–4.
(footnote *f*)		
87	42	*L.-Bk. I*, p. 267; *L.-Bk. K*, p. 267.
87	43	Beaven, Part I, p. 332.
87	44	*L.-Bk. H*, p. 310.
87	45	*L.-Bk. G*, p. 203.
87	46	*L.-Bk. H*, p. 310.
88	47	Ibid., p. 277.
88	48	„ p. 336. Dr Sharpe points out that the proceedings in this Parliament are not recorded on the Rolls (Introduction, p. xlviii, footnote 3).
88	49	Ibid., pp. 226, 247, 249, 274.
88	50	*English Gilds*, by Toulmin Smith, pp. 127–31.
88	51	*L.-Bk. H*, p. 193.
89	52	*Pl. & M. Rolls*, 1381–1412, pp. 148–9.
89	53	*English Gilds*, op. cit., pp. 133–4.
89	54	*L.-Bk. H*, p. 384; *P.R.*, 1388–92, pp. 321–2.
89	55	A précis of this Charter is given in *Records of the Skinners of London, Edw. I to James I*, by J. J. Lambert, pp. 50–2.
89	56	See *P.R.*, 1391–6, p. 219. The letters patent are dated 6th February 1394.
89	57	Ibid., pp. 425–6.
89	58	„ p. 560.
90	59	See *An Account of the Mistery of Mercers of the City of London, otherwise the Mercers Company* (1914) compiled by Sir John Watney, F.S.A., p. 37.
(footnote *j*)		
90	60	*L.-Bk. H*, p. 402.
90	61	Ibid., p. 416.
90	62	*An Account of the Mistery of Mercers*, op. cit., p. 37.
(footnote *k*)		
90	63	*L.-Bk. I*, p. 109.
90	64	*C.W.C.H.*, Part II, pp. 403–4, Roll 142 (13).
90	65	Ibid., p. 369, Roll 134 (77).

Page	Note	
90	66	*Husting Rolls* (101–25) 123.18.126 (1395).
90	67	Ibid. (126–75) 129. dors. 114 (1401).
91	68	*C.W.C.H.*, Part II, p. 361, Roll 133 (63).
91	69	*L.-Bk. I*, p. 49.
91	70	*Husting Rolls* (101–25) 110.12.116 (1382).
91	71	*C.W.C.H.*, Part II, p. 348, Roll 129 (29).
91	72	*L.-Bk. H*, pp. 34–5.
91	73	Ibid., p. 391.
91 (footnote *n*)	74	,, p. 381.
91	75	*Husting Rolls* (101–25) 123.4.31 (1394).
91	76	*L.-Bk. I*, p. 65.
91	77	Ibid., p. 8.
92	78	*Husting Rolls* (101–25) 123.1.4 (1394).
92	79	*L.-Bk. I*, p. 172.
92	80	*Pl. & M. Rolls*, 1381–1412, p. 127.
92	81	*Pl. & M. Rolls*, 1413–37, pp. 282–3.
93	82	See *The Turbulent London of Richard II* by Ruth Bird, pp. 52–6, and the Table in Appendix III.
93	83	See *L.-Bk. H*, pp. 245–6 and footnote.
93	84	*Pl. & M. Rolls*, 1381–1412, p. 57.
93	85	Ibid., pp. 58–60.
93 (footnote *p*)	86	See *L.-Bk. H*, p. 266 (footnote).
93	87	Ibid., pp. 264–6.
93	88	,, p. 250.
93	89	,, p. 251.
94	90	*Pl. & M. Rolls*, 1381–1412, pp. 62–3.
94	91	Ibid., pp. 63–9.
94	92	See Cobbett's *State Trials*, edition of 1809, Vol. I, pp. 89–124.
95	93	Higden, *Polychron*, IX, pp. 270, 272–3; Walsingham, *Hist. Angl.*, II, pp. 208–9. (See *London and the Kingdom* by Dr R. R. Sharpe, Vol. I, pp. 240–2.)

Page	Note	
95	94	L.-Bk. H, p. 379.
95	95	Letter describing Richard II's reconciliation with the City of London 1392, printed in *The English Historical Review*, Vol. LXII, 1947, pp. 209–13.
95	96	See the account in *London and the Kingdom* by Dr R. R. Sharpe, Vol. I, pp. 244–5.
96 (footnote *w*)	97	*The Fifteenth Century, 1399–1485* by E. F. Jacob, pp. 11–14.
96	98	See *London and the Kingdom*, op. cit., Vol. I, p. 245, quoting Froissart (*Chronicles*, Bk. IV).
96	99	*The Fourteenth Century, 1307–1399*, op. cit., p. 496.

APPENDICES

Appendix	Note	
A	1	See *A Dictionary of London* by Henry A. Harben (1918), p. 603. The author's statement that the stream entered the City 'to the east of Cripplegate' is somewhat misleading.
	2	*A Dictionary of London*, op. cit., p. 605.
(footnote *a*)		
	3	Ibid., p. 165.
B		E.M.C.R., (1) p. 2, (2) p. 6, (3) p. 23, (4) p. 74, (5) p. 189, (6) pp. 86–7, (7) p. 124, (8) p. 154, (9) pp. 110–11.
C		L.-Bk. C, p. 11.
D. 1		L.-Bk. B, pp. 265–6.
D. 2		L.-Bk. A, pp. 158–9.
E		L.-Bk. D, pp. 24–6.
F		Riley, *Memorials*, p. 225.
G		*Pl. & M. Rolls*, 1364–81, pp. 158–9.
H		Riley, *Memorials*, p. 265.
I		Ibid., pp. 300–2.

Appendix	*Note*	
J		*L.-Bk. G*, pp. 171–2.
K		31st July 1384: *L.-Bk. H*, pp. 237–40.
		August 1384: *L.-Bk. H*, p. 245.
		13th October 1384: *Pl. & M. Rolls*, 1381–1412, pp. 84–8.
		1384/5: Ibid., pp. 91–2.
		18th July 1385: *L.-Bk. H*, pp. 269–71.
		1385/6: *Pl. & M. Rolls*, 1381–1412, pp. 122–4.
		March 1386: *L.-Bk. H*, pp. 279–82.
		1387: *Pl. & M. Rolls*, 1381–1412, pp. 132–3.
		31st August 1388: *L.-Bk. H*, pp. 322–34.
L	1	*L.-Bk. H*, pp. 403, 413, 418.
	2	Ibid., p. 403.
	3	*L.-Bk. I*, p. 147.
	4	Ibid., p. 172.
	5	„ pp. 212–13.
	6	*C.W.C.H.*, Part II, p. 452, Roll 159 (8).
	7	Index to *Testamentary Records*, op. cit., p. 8.
	8	*Husting Rolls* (101–25) 115. dors. 22 (1386).
	9	*C.W.C.H.*, Part II, p. 330, Roll 126 (54).

Index

Figures in italics indicate footnotes